Bright Swallow

BRIGHT SWALLOW

MAKING CHOICES IN MAO'S CHINA: A MEMOIR

VIVIAN BI

HYBRID PUBLISHERS

Published by Hybrid Publishers

Melbourne Victoria Australia

www.hybridpublishers.com.au

First published 2019

A catalogue record for this
book is available from the
National Library of Australia

ISBN 9781925736106 (p)

9781925736120 (e)

Cover design: Gittus Graphics www.gggraphics.com.au

Contents

What should a person's life be likened to?
To a wild goose treading on mushy snow
Who leaves its random footprints behind.
When it flies away the wild goose does not deliberate.

– Su Shi (1037–1101), "Remembering the Past"

1

A Mother's Challenge

September 1972 was a happy month for me, because my mother had lung cancer. I hate to say those words but it's the truth. I was too young to know the seriousness of the disease and her illness eased my daily hardship.

On 13 August 1972, my fifteenth birthday, my next-door neighbour Mrs Han called me into her house. She had cooked me a birthday dinner of a "lion's head" (a big meatball) on top of a bowl of longevity noodles. My mother, Yukang, was in another province, visiting her sister, so I was alone at our Beijing home. Of course, I was not really alone as my mother had asked Mrs Han and other neighbours to look after me for these few days.

I sat down in front of my special meal and grinned from ear to ear. The noodles were typical birthday fare but it was the "lion's head" that was the really pleasant surprise. In those days, a pure meat dish like this could only be expected during the New Year festival.

I knew I had been a good girl while my mother was away, washing myself every day, keeping the house tidy and dutifully doing my holiday homework. This must be my reward. Feeling proud of myself, I took my first bite of the "lion's head". Then I noticed that no one else – not Mr and Mrs Han nor their grown-up children – was eating. "Sorry, I should have waited," I apologised as I put down my chopsticks.

Mrs Han then told me of my mother's diagnosis. "She asked me to let you know," she said gently, "so you'd be prepared when she gets back."

It was the first time I had heard of cancer. I gathered from the sad looks on everyone's faces that it must be bad. So *this* was the reason for the "lion's head". I didn't know how to react. I sat bolt upright until Mrs Han said, "Eat before the food gets cold."

Two days later, my mother returned from her visit to her sister, my Aunt Yuqin, who was a surgeon in a small city. Aunt Yuqin had made the diagnosis during my mother's visit and urged my mother to return to Beijing for a thorough examination. My mother's brother, my Uncle Yuji, was a thoracic specialist in Beijing and he immediately organised for her to be examined at the Beijing Cancer Hospital, where the diagnosis was confirmed. Not only that, but my mother was told she had only two months to live.

At that time, my father was still living in exile in Jiayuguan, a town in the Gobi Desert. A "bad element" in the eyes of the Communist government, he had been sent there in 1965 for an indefinite period, and my five older brothers, "children of bad origins", had been dispatched to factories or villages in remote parts of the country. Because I was still at school, I had been allowed to stay in Beijing for the time being.

Since I was the only one living with my mother, Uncle Yuji decided that rather than go back to school in the September semester I should remain at home to be by my mother's side. He told me that once the cancer advanced to her nervous system, she would be paralysed.

It was all a bit overwhelming and I couldn't really take in what it all meant, but I was happy that I did not have to go to school, because before the summer vacation I had been bullied by a classmate named Ling.

Ling was disabled. Her mother had been working in a factory when she'd fallen pregnant. Ling told us that, not wanting to lose her job, her mother had tried to hide her pregnancy by strapping a tight belt around her belly. Ling said that this was why she had been born with a left arm that ended at the elbow, a right hand with only a thumb and stumps for fingers, and no toes on her feet.

She had joined our school in Year 8. On her first day, a boy rushed into the classroom and announced that we had a new classmate, an "armless cripple". Before he'd finished describing the "cripple", Ling came into the room, walking awkwardly with her weight thrown back on her heels. She went directly up to the boy and stared intently at him. Everyone watched as he shrank down behind his desk.

Two years on, Ling had won the respect of the entire class for her extraordinary capability and her tough manner. She was not only able to look after herself, she knitted sweaters for her parents and even embroidered pillowcases. She showed us how, wedging one knitting needle in the crook of her left elbow and holding it in place with what little forearm she had, or using her feet to hold the embroidery hoop while she stitched with her one "good" hand. No one dared tease or displease her "intentionally", as she put it, because she would exact ruthless revenge and organise the whole class to attack her tormentor.

I had admired Ling's fighting spirit and understood that she had to be tough. I had befriended her and we had visited each other's homes and sometimes walked to school together. So it was a shock when in early July, after the end of the semester exams, she suddenly stopped talking to me and ordered others to shun me.

Although we were in the middle of the decade-long Cultural Revolution (1966–76), 1972 was a year of relative calm. A year earlier, Chairman Mao's hand-picked successor, Lin Biao, had been labelled an assassin and a traitor to the nation. His failed coup rattled Mao for a while, allowing more moderate leaders to re-establish some order in the country. One outcome was that academic achievement was suddenly important again, and we had test after test and exam after exam. Ling studied furiously, wanting to be number one at everything, but I still came out on top, so she set out to undermine me, seemingly the only obstacle to her aspirations.

I had inherited my father's photographic memory. His nickname was Library Bi, because he was able to remember everything he read. My father enjoyed showing off his extraordinary memory. When I was little he would order me to pick a book from the shelf, open it at random and read the first line. He would then recite the rest of the page. My memory was far inferior to his, but when I was confronted with exam papers I could see the answers in my textbook or notebook, on the exact lines and pages, which enabled me to achieve high marks.

The last two weeks of that school semester were miserable. Ling made sure no one spoke to me. When she walked past me, she'd deliberately bump into me, hard. On the final day, I found a note inside my desk drawer: "If you don't mend your ways, you'll be sorted out in September." I shivered when I read it. I fled home, burnt the note and tried to forget about it, but for the entire vacation it loomed over me like a nightmare.

So when Uncle Yuji told me I did not have to go back to school, I was over the moon and secretly thanked my mother for having cancer.

Another pleasant surprise in September 1972 was that my mother made me my first-ever brand-new shirt. She was an excellent seamstress and had made me many garments, but none were actually new. I had trousers in Polish wool, made from her overcoat; and silk dresses, rayon blouses and satin underwear, made from her old mandarin gowns. Every time she asked me to try on another "new" garment, I put on a long face and slouched uncooperatively. I nagged her to make me blue cotton trousers and a white cotton shirt, like the ones my classmates wore, but she had no money for that and criticised me for having no taste and for being ungrateful.

I knew that, because of my "bad origins", I could not be a "normal girl". But I wanted to blend in at school and hated being conspicuous in my dowdy old clothes. So I resented my mother and the family I had been born into.

My mother had her own frustrations and resentments too. One day I had a fall on the way to school and tore my Polish wool trousers. I came home crying, my knees covered in blood, but all she said was, "You have to get what you want at any cost, don't you?"

I stopped crying immediately. When she tried to clean my broken skin with cotton pads and anti-inflammatory lotion I pushed her hands away and did it myself. I fought back tears, avoided looking at her and left for school, still wearing the torn trousers. As soon as I got out on the street, I cried with grief and indignation. For me, this was confirmation yet again that my mother didn't love me.

I was the youngest of six and the only girl of the family. My mother was forty-six when I was born and had been trying to have a girl for more than a decade. As soon as I slipped out of her body, she lifted her head and asked eagerly, "Boy or girl?"

The doctors and nurses of the Sixth Hospital of Beijing assumed that she must be one of those older women who were desperate to have a son. To avoid distressing her so soon after giving birth, a nurse told her, "A boy, of course."

According to my father, my mother fell back and said, "Give him away!"

She was overjoyed when they told her the truth. "I've waited all these years and finally I've been blessed by Heaven," she said to everyone who visited her in hospital. She and my father named me Xiyan, which means "Bright Swallow", swallows symbolising spring, freedom and the future. But her happiness was short-lived. A few months after I was born, my father became one of the 550,000 officially recorded Rightists and had a 50 per cent pay cut. In addition, as his wife, my mother was "advised to resign" from the work force. She often said that in the old society I would have been considered a bad omen, because after I was born things began to fall apart. Her words made me feel unwanted. I would try to make myself invisible when I was with her because I believed I was an annoyance. Indeed, in the fifteen years of my life with her, I seldom saw her smile.

That September, between her frequent visits to hospital, my mother made a new shirt for me. It was cotton, with irregular blue checks on a white background. When I put it on and stood in front of the mirror, I was delighted to see that finally I looked like everyone else. I wore the new shirt almost every day from then on.

It was not only the shirt, though. My mother became much nicer to me. Perhaps she wanted to give me as much love and care as she could before her time ran out. The disapproval I had often seen on her face disappeared and my habit of tiptoeing around her while assessing her mood became unnecessary.

She was having radiotherapy three times a week. She was exhausted after every session and would sit down to recover while I paid the bill at the cashier, or made the next booking at the registration window. She often said to me apologetically, "You shouldn't be here in the first place. I'm so sorry."

When she did not have to go to the hospital, she would do her best to put tempting dishes on the table for me. One day after dinner, she placed a plate with a bowl on top of it in front of me. "What's this?"

"Have a look," my mother said, smiling affectionately.

I lifted the bowl and to my wonderment I saw two sesame cakes, a rather expensive snack.

"The doctor said I didn't need the second X-ray, so I thought this would be the best way to use some of the money we saved."

I stared at the cakes for a while, then put one of them in front of her, but she pushed it back onto my plate. "I don't have much of an appetite so this good thing would just be wasted. You enjoy it."

I finished one in no time then asked carefully, "Should I leave the second one for tomorrow?"

"Finish it off if you like." She watched me enjoy it with an even broader smile.

I felt spoiled during that month and reciprocated her extra care by being on my best behaviour. I'd take the initiative to sweep the floor, put the dishes away or make the beds. I even began to talk to her about how I was being bullied at school. She told me to be strong and to be myself, and assured me that the bullies wouldn't last long. I enjoyed being with her.

In September 1972, I also had more time to spend with friends. From the age of ten, I had helped my mother look after the baby of my oldest brother, Yang, and then the baby of my second-oldest brother,

Shu. While other kids were having fun I had to babysit, which earned me the nickname Child Mother.

One day, I was supposed to be looking after my sixteen-month-old nephew at home while my mother went shopping for dinner. Instead I took him to the playground in Beihai Park with the other kids. I set him down against the fence and went off to play on the swings and slippery dips, and in the cubby houses. I was having a good time until someone called out that my nephew had his head stuck between the fence railings. The more he struggled to pull his head free, the deeper his head became wedged. He was screaming so hard he was turning purple. A couple of the older kids tried to bend the fence rails out while the younger ones just joined in with my nephew's screaming. It was absolute mayhem.

We finally had to call the park rangers and then firemen to free him. I was very frightened, worrying about my nephew's head and how my mother would react. Fortunately, my nephew survived with just a few scratches but my mother was furious. "What if something had happened to the baby? You think I like to do this, look after someone else's child! I do it to feed you."

She told me afterwards that, in addition to his original blemish of being labelled a Rightist in 1957, my father had committed another "horrible crime" – distorting a Chairman Mao quotation in public. As was the fashion then, he had scrawled the Chairman Mao quotation "Never forget class struggle!" on the back of a letter he posted home from the Gobi Desert. The word "forget" is formed by two characters – 忘 (forget) and 记 (remember) – so the phrase is literally "Never forget to remember class struggle." My father left out the character 忘, so the quote read "Never remember class struggle." Thanks to the postman, who had clearly never forgotten class struggle, my father received a new title: "active reactionary". He was put under higher-level control and had his salary cancelled altogether. We were now living on a stipend of 30 yuan per month – equivalent to five dollars – from my father's company. This would not cover our rent, electricity and water bills, and daily expenses.

To make the 30 yuan last, my mother and I ate rough cornbread every day. I remember at one meal I put down the cornbread and begged my mother to make me a couple of wheat buns. She looked at me, blinked back a tear, and said, "Be satisfied that you have something to fill your belly. If your father keeps making mistakes, you might miss even cornmeal bread one day." I shut up and picked up the cornbread. I didn't want to starve.

My mother did her best to economise. On the day she received the 30-yuan allowance, she would stock up on the staples of flour and rice for the month. "At least we won't starve," she would say. She would go to the co-op in the late afternoon, when there were usually discounted vegetables. A lifelong tea connoisseur, she bought high quality tea dust for next to nothing to satisfy her refined tastes. She even rationed her letters. A stamp cost eight fen (cents) and since she couldn't afford the cost of stamps for two letters a month to her husband and five sons, she wrote in small characters on many sheets of thin paper and posted letters to everyone only once a month.

Counting every cent squeezed out all other concerns. We lived in a big residential compound in the heart of Beijing, between Beihai Park and Jingshan Park, the two imperial gardens next to the Forbidden City. When our family, along with thirty-two other families, moved into this government-provided multi-courtyard housing compound in the early 1950s, my parents had chosen the best house. It was located in the front courtyard, at the top of five marble steps and with a deep front veranda and an enclosed back garden which connected to the rear courtyard. It was also the biggest in the compound, with two large front rooms and one double-sized room at the back. Its windows were of etched glass, the floor of tessellated tiles. Naturally, it was the most expensive: at 9.80 yuan per month, the rent was almost four times that of the average house.

Back then, my parents had been in a privileged position. My father, a graduate of the Northern Institute of Technology (China's first Western-style college, established in 1895 by the Guangxu Emperor), had been employed by the new Communist government as one of its "progressive intellectuals". He was working on major hydraulic and architectural projects such as the Thirteen Tombs Dam and the Ten Grand Constructions, both monumental projects of Mao's China.

My mother had also been accepted as a "progressive intellectual" and worked for the same construction company as my father. She belonged to the first generation of Chinese women with a college degree so she had been employed as a union leader, in charge of organising entertainment to boost workers' morale.

Their combined monthly income of 230 yuan was four or five times that of the average household, so they could afford the best house with a garden.

In 1969, Chairman Mao instructed everyone to dig air-raid shelters on campuses, courtyards and streets to protect themselves against "imminent invasion" from the Soviet Union. Our neighbours came together, dug a hole four metres by ten metres in the middle of the outer yard, lined it with bricks, covered it with timber, put entrances at each end, and concealed it with turf. Since all the materials had to be sourced locally, the wall and the gate of our back garden were torn down.

The damage to our traditional compound and the loss of my family's garden didn't concern us much – we were following Chairman Mao's instructions, which could not be questioned. But I shared my mother's huge disappointment that our rent was not reduced accordingly. "If only we could have two more yuan for food …" my mother would often say, while I nodded in agreement. Since the government controlled all housing, moving to a less expensive house was not an option.

In such tough circumstances, looking after my brother's baby earned my mother an extra 30 yuan a month, the fee my brother would otherwise be paying for day care, and with that we could get along a bit better.

However, once my mother got cancer, there was no more looking after the baby. Now I was not woken night after night by the baby's crying, and I could go out to play with the neighbourhood kids whenever I liked.

My mother's treatment was costly and to this day I don't know who paid for it. Uncle Yuji perhaps? Someone must have been helping because that September our living conditions were better than usual.

My job of keeping my mother company was easy. Uncle Yuji reminded me constantly not to leave her alone, but to me she seemed all right. She still did all the housework and when she rested, she wrote letters or read books while I had fun out on the street with the other kids.

Roller-skating was popular at the time and I was keen on it. I didn't have my own skates so I'd wait to borrow someone else's skates when they took a break. I had to wait for hours sometimes. Once my mother said, "Can't you stay home and spend some time with me?" Seeing me standing there with head bowed and saying nothing, she waved her hand and said, "Go, go enjoy yourself."

I knew I should stay home and I felt guilty. But all that was soon forgotten when I was zooming about on the skates.

Another treat that month was wandering around the different co-ops collecting free fruit. A big storm in early September had destroyed most of the orchards. The damaged apples, pears and persimmons were distributed to Beijing's co-ops to sell cheaply. Fruit was a luxury for ordinary people. It was seen as the privilege of the rich or only for the sick. But that September everyone could buy a huge bundle of apples for three or five fen. And that was not all. At the end of the day, there were often free leftovers. I hauled back so much fruit that, after washing it, cutting off the rotten bits and eating it, my teeth became too sensitive to continue. But I felt like one of the fortunate rich.

On the last day of September, I returned home with a load of sugar pears. "Mum, look what I've got."

There was no response.

I put the pears on the table in the living room and ran into her room. My mother sat in bed, sobbing. Alarmed, I sat down next to her.

Through her tears she asked, "What are you going to do without me?"

I rarely spoke of my feelings, but at that moment I felt I must say something because I knew what she was referring to. I hesitated, for I was going to touch on a taboo topic. "Mum, is it about Old Mushroom? Don't worry. I'll steer clear of her."

Old Mushroom was my father's first wife. We gave her this nickname as a double pun. The Chinese word for "mushroom" is pronounced exactly like the word for "bother", and "old" can also mean "forever". This woman was another reason for my habitually cautious behaviour around my mother.

The son of a traditional family, my father had married at sixteen and became a father at seventeen. He left home to study and pursued his career while his illiterate wife stayed at home, looking after his parents and raising a son and two daughters. When the war with Japan broke out in the late 1930s, he lost contact with his family. It was rumoured that his wife and children might have died in an air raid so he married my mother, whom he had met in an amateur opera theatre group. That was in 1938. One year later, his wife reappeared. Although the Kuomintang government had instituted monogamy, the fine print of the law said that, concubinage being a 2000-year-old tradition, there was no need to insist on the practice "too rigidly".

In 1952, my father brought his first family to Beijing, and Old Mushroom had remained there to "bother" us ever since. She lived nearby, hung around my family and whenever possible would send her grown-up daughters – my half-sisters – to our house to smash things. She herself would smack me or kick me whenever she came across me out playing. She would grab me by the collar and demand that I call her "mother" – "Your mother is not a mother. She's only a concubine." Then my mother would add her own slap and blame me for going near the woman. So I would often feel more angry with her than with Old Mushroom – "Some mother!" I would think.

Over time, my resentment was gradually redirected to my father as the cause of the mess. I tried to stay away from Old Mushroom to avoid creating trouble for myself and for my mother, who preferred to close her eyes to the other woman's existence.

Hearing me confidently say that I could manage Old Mushroom, my mother smiled wryly. "I'm afraid it won't be so easy for you to walk away anymore." While I was still digesting this, she wiped away her tears and asked me to set the table for dinner. "Put your sugar pears in a saucepan and go wash them."

I went to the public tap in the yard to wash the pears. When I finished, she had dinner on the table and had sat down. During dinner, she began to talk to me.

My mother liked to talk. Never gossip, but rather her opinions on life. For example, when she taught me to sew, she would say that clothes were worn for oneself, not for others, so underwear must be of the best quality. After she cleaned the house, she would make a cup of tea, light a cigarette, sit down with a book and point out how nice it was to enjoy clean surroundings. She would also discuss current affairs with our neighbours, literature and Beijing opera with my father, and music with my brothers. I would listen to her calm and eloquent pronouncements attentively and feel how different she seemed from other mothers. She, however, often referred to me as a mute mule – wordless and stubborn – and wondered whose genes I had inherited, because both she and my father were talkers. According to her, all my father's misfortunes were caused by his "big mouth".

Her favourite topics were clothes and adventure. In clothes, she preferred the simple and natural. She had a mandarin dress made of georgette with thin yellow stripes on a navy-blue background. When I turned ten, she made me a pleated skirt out of it. I did not like it because at the time young girls were wearing red or hot pink dresses with bubbled shoulders.

When she saw my long face, she gave me my first lesson on style.

She took out from the sideboard a blue plate patterned after the Ming dynasty and a multi-coloured mug in the manner of the Qing. "Which one do you like?"

I pointed to the mug.

Shaking her head, she said, "Beauty exists in simplicity, and taste is reflected in subtlety."

Then she told me how Chinese civilisation had reached its peak in the Ming dynasty so the Ming design represented confidence and elegance. On the other hand, the designs of the Manchurian rulers of Qing were saturated with the vulgarity of the nouveau riche.

"Red or hot pink is not the colour for your darker complexion and bubble shoulders not only make you shorter but also look cheap and showy, just like this," she pointed to the mug.

My mother regarded life as an adventure full of risks that were there to be taken. "When I decided to marry your father, I knew it wouldn't be easy but I went ahead." She told me this during one of her hospital visits. "If you know the risks and prepare well beforehand, trouble or danger can be avoided while your life becomes fuller. You see, I travelled everywhere with your father, experienced plenty of extraordinary things, and had all you children," she concluded with a sigh.

On that last night of September 1972, her topic was death.

My mother had talked to me about death before, because death was a common topic in those years. After the Cultural Revolution started in 1966, many "class enemies" were ferreted out. Some were executed by the government or beaten to death by the Red Guards; others committed suicide out of despair. Since we lived near the Beihai and Jingshan parks, we frequently heard of people drowning themselves in Beihai Lake or hanging themselves on Jingshan Peak. In our compound alone, two neighbours from the rear courtyard – a female teacher and a male dentist – had killed themselves.

I didn't know these two neighbours. The local revolutionary committee announced afterwards that these were the deaths of enemies and, quoting the newspapers, called it “gratifying news”. Along with the many other youngsters in the compound, I had simply accepted this, until the summer of 1971.

In May and June of that year, Beijingers were frequently marching against either American imperialists or Soviet Union revisionists. One such march took place on an early summer’s day. Exhausted after five hours of marching and shouting slogans, I was returning home with two girls from my class who lived in a long winding laneway called Dashizuo, which led to my street. When we arrived at one girl’s house, she said goodbye and disappeared inside. My friend and I walked on, but before we had passed the next yard, the other girl rushed out, screaming hysterically. Her mother had hanged herself.

We had known her mother as an elegant woman who lectured at a university. We’d often dropped in to collect our friend on our way to school. The mother had always smiled at us and sometimes given us candies or biscuits too. I found it hard to imagine this woman as a “class enemy”. While the authorities declared her death the elimination of yet another enemy, my classmate was inconsolable. I felt miserable too and thought about the two neighbours, and their children’s grief. I could no longer see death as gratifying. Death was horrible.

After this incident, many of us were scared to go home. Anyone in our family could be an enemy who might commit suicide. For days, I would first peep inside the house from the veranda. If I did not see my mother in the front room, I would call out loudly until she came out. Finally, she sat me down. “You don’t need to do that. I won’t kill myself. Death is not an easy thing to achieve and I …” she paused, “I’m a coward.” I was not sure at all about her self-portrayal, but I was happy to know that she would not kill herself.

My mother’s talk often received a silent reception from me, but on this night, when she talked about death, I tried to engage in the conversation.

She told me she had cheated death twice. After giving birth to my third-oldest brother she had been bleeding heavily and heard the doctor announce her imminent demise, but she proved him wrong. Another time she was on a plane to Chongqing and an engine failed. The passengers were asked to write wills, but she refused and in the end the plane landed safely. "You see," she looked at me beseechingly, "I might be able to do it again."

I nodded, "Yes, Mum. Chairman Mao says if you are determined and not afraid to die, you will be victorious." My response was so natural because we had been trained to think and talk this way.

She looked away and began to clear the table. I could see she was not pleased by what I had said but I had no idea why.

Afterwards, I bathed and changed in the back room while she sat on a stool washing my new shirt in the living room, as she had done every night that month.

"I wish I had had enough money to make you two shirts," she said. Once again she mentioned another piece of fabric she had wanted to buy for me. "It's pretty, with golden bamboo leaves on a light jade background and a smattering of tiny red berries."

I responded, "It's fine, Mum. I like this one, blue and white, everyone wears these colours. I don't want to look like a bourgeois."

She said nothing in reply. I poured the dirty water into the public drain and hung the shirt on the clothes line. When I came back, she was still sitting on the stool. "Do you need me to help you get up?"

"No. I'm fine. I'm waiting for you to cut up some pear for me."

Cheerfully, I trimmed the bad pieces off the fruit I had brought home and presented it to her. I did not do a good job as many pieces still tasted bad. She picked up a couple and gave up. "When I was your age, I was told it was better to taste a single mouthful of fresh peach than eat a basketful of old apricots."

"But, Mum, I have never eaten so much fruit." I stumbled on, saying, "Today at the co-op, I ate ten sugar pears in one go. One boy from the outer yard ate nineteen …"

My mother cut me short, saying she was tired and wanted to turn in early. I noticed she struggled to get up and walked awkwardly. I asked her if she was okay.

"I had a fall this afternoon, but I'm okay," she replied. Then she turned to me as she entered her room. "You know what? I feel happy now. At least I've lived a life."

I did not know that her fall was a sign of the cancer attacking her nervous system and the beginning of the end. I learnt this the hard way the next morning when I woke to find she could no longer walk or talk. I was horrified to see her struggle to lift her hand and to utter unintelligible sounds. Her eyes were filled with despair. I didn't know what to do. "Mum, Mum!" I cried out. "What happened to you?" The neighbours rushed in and sent me to the public telephone to call my uncle. Suddenly I realised that her death was not just predicted; it was an imminent reality.

Whenever I think back to our last conversation, I feel such pity for a dying mother who wanted so much for her only daughter. How painful it must have been to hear her daughter's ignorant pronouncements on life. Worse, after enduring Mao's class struggles for two decades, she must have foreseen a bleak future for her "bad origins" daughter, a life of suppression, a life bereft of choices. Her life, disrupted as it had been, had been a rich one, a life with choices. She had been properly educated, she had had adventures, and she had, at one time, enjoyed daily comforts and success in her career. *She* had lived a life!

2

Grief and Defiance

Fighting back my tears, I ran to the public telephone at the end of the street to ring Uncle Yuji. It was 1 October, China's National Day and a public holiday. The local children were playing in the street as the crowds poured in to tour the imperial gardens. I kept my head down as I passed through the happy crowd, feeling cheated. *Why does mother have to have cancer and why do I have to deal with all of this?* I was fifteen years old.

Uncle Yuji arrived an hour later. He held my mother's hand and cried a little, then dashed out to telegraph my father and brothers. My fourth-oldest brother, Dong, rushed back that evening. He was distraught and kept saying to me, "Do you know Mum can't talk or move anymore?" as if I was the one who had just arrived home. Dong was the only one of my brothers to have kept his valuable Beijing registration, but he had been assigned to a full-time job in the propaganda team of the Ministry of Industrial Electronics. He was an actor in political shows and set up exhibitions nationwide, so he had been away from home for years.

My second-oldest brother, Shu, returned from Xi'an two days later. He started crying even before he got in the front door. Dong and I had to stop him going into Mother's bedroom until he calmed down. We didn't want to further upset her.

Shu had acted as the head of the family after my father was exiled to Gobi. It had been his idea to help my mother financially by having her look after two of her grandsons. As soon as he collected himself, he began to deal with the challenge of finding the money to bring my third-oldest brother, Ning, and my youngest brother, Jing, home.

Jing was being "re-educated" in the far northeast, working as a farmer in a remote village and struggling to earn enough to feed himself.

In June 1966 when Chairman Mao started the Cultural Revolution, he abolished the academic merit-based examinations. "They are the dregs of feudalism and capitalism, and discriminate against the proletariat," he claimed. As a result, senior high schools and universities were closed and students and graduates were urged to make revolution.

Two years later, however, Mao realised that millions of idle youngsters were not only a huge burden on the scarce supplies in the cities but were also potential trouble. He issued a new "supreme instruction" at the end of 1968: all the young people whose minds and bodies had been damaged by the old school system must go to the countryside to be re-educated by "the poor and lower-middle peasants". Within a year, tens of thousands of city youths, one-tenth of Beijing's population, streamed out of the city, Jing among them.

Jing had just turned sixteen and could have delayed his departure for up to a year, but our mother decided it would be good for him to leave Beijing before his reckless nature landed him in serious trouble.

Despite his "bad origins", Jing, like me, wanted to blend in with the masses. While my dream was limited to a new shirt, his was to join the Red Guards, where he could bully others and have fun in the name of revolution. My mother scolded him with the old saying, "Not knowing how high the sky is and how thick the earth is", that is, being hopelessly naive. The Red Guard slogan was: "Hero fathers bear good sons and reactionaries bear skunks", and membership was restricted to proletarian families.

Stubborn and foolhardy, Jing had secretly organised a group of youngsters who shared his frustrations and who saw him as their leader. They hung around together and often got into street fights. My mother worried that if people noticed the group's "tainted" background, they would soon find themselves in serious trouble. She had to do something to redirect their energy.

She had bought Jing an *erhu*, a two-stringed violin, and offered to teach the whole group how to play this traditional instrument. And so, with the support of other anxious parents, an *erhu* group was formed. That was how I learnt Mum had been a musician. I wished I knew her better but didn't dare ask questions because she had taught us not to speak out of turn. Now, seeing her teaching and playing so excellently, she was shrouded in even more mystery.

She was a strict teacher, and the idle youngsters were eager learners. Before long, they could play many traditional *erhu* tunes and when ten instruments played in unison they drew large audiences from the neighbourhood. Enthralled, I asked to join the class but my mother would not allow me to mingle with this group of "wild boys".

Yet, trouble was inevitable for Jing. At the end of 1968, for example, the ballet "Red Detachment of Women", one of the eight Revolutionary Model Operas approved and produced by Mao's wife Jiang Qing, was being performed and, hungry for entertainment, young people, Jing's group among them, had rushed to the box office and queued for tickets for two days and nights in the cold. On the third day, a hysterical Jing came back home to get a kitchen knife. His group had been kicked out of the queue at the last minute because they were not Red Guards. My mother chased him down the street, pleading with him to come back while I stood at the front of the house, crying in fear. Jing did come back but he smashed a stool in his room. Then I understood why my mother called Jing "wild".

Shu managed to send funds to Jing for his rail ticket and he got home on 10 October. Mum's eyes lit up as soon as he walked in. She could not talk, but was obviously pleased to see her baby son looking grown up and strong.

My mother had to wait another five long days to see Ning, my third-oldest brother. Ning was a lost boy who had been sent to reform school at seventeen for boasting, lying, and not paying for meals in restaurants. He paid a big price for these petty crimes when he was exiled to Xinjiang, the New Territory on the border of China and the Soviet Union.

Early in 1965, when the Communist government began the campaign to develop the great northwest, the first group of Beijing "volunteers" came from the reform schools. Ning was assigned to Turpan, in the south of Xinjiang, a relatively desirable destination. Two special trains were assigned to deliver these troubled youngsters there a month apart and my mother opted for the second train for her son, wanting to hold on to him as long as possible. But in one of the carriages in the second train were hard-core criminals under armed escort, and when the train passed through Henan province, they overpowered their escort and hijacked the train in protest against their exile. After three days of rioting, they were executed on the spot, and in a bid to suppress this bad news, the remaining passengers were sent on to the farthest and poorest location in Xinjiang, Khashgar.

As my mother entered the final week of her life, my job was guarding her in the front bedroom. When Ning arrived home after a seven-year absence, I thought he was a beggar and in a panic called out for Shu. Ning was smelly and dirty and his clothes were in tatters, but my mother had no trouble recognising her son. Her grief was palpable when she touched him with the only fingers she could still move. Ning was sobbing and I joined him. I felt my mother's longing and despair. When Shu rushed in from the back room, he cried too.

Yang, my oldest brother, returned from Sichuan the same day. He had not been home for three years and had not communicated with any of the family. During the Cultural Revolution, plenty of children broke off contact with their parents. One of the slogans targeting those of "bad class" origins was: "You can't choose your family origin but you can decide your class standard." However, in our family it was my mother who had severed relations with Yang.

Yang was her most cultivated son. He was a published poet and songwriter, and he played piano and accordion. But he was a weak man who, according to my mother, would avoid trouble at any cost. He left home in 1958 as part of the campaign to develop the great northern wilderness, working first as a farmer and then as a technician in the Harbin Turbine Factory. Seven years later he was transferred to Sichuan and became a purchasing agent for the construction of the Oriental Turbine Factory.

Yang longed to return to Beijing, so he married a Beijing rickshaw-puller's daughter, hoping this proletarian connection would be the means by which he could come back. Normally, the sons of scholars did not marry the daughters of labourers, but during the Cultural Revolution families of "bad origins" sought protection while proletarians sought status by intermarrying.

My mother did not approve of the marriage. "The most important thing in a marriage is family background," she told him. "You can marry a cleaner from a cultivated family but not a professor from a peasant household." My brother told his fiancée what his mother had said and the next evening, her father, the rickshaw puller, appeared in our yard. A bald, shirtless man, he stood there cursing my mother's ancestors for eight generations for a full hour. His parting shot was: "Only I have the right to say yes or no to this marriage because it is your son, a toad, who is lusting after my swan's flesh."

In the end, the toad married the swan.

Before her wedding, my future sister-in-law tried to get closer to my mother through me. One day she visited us in full Red Guard splendour and invited me to join her in a raid on an old bourgeois lady's home. My mother slapped me in front of her, hissing, "Don't you dare!"

I was so shocked, I talked back – something I had never done. "I didn't say I'd go," I mumbled and ran into my room.

My mother knocked on my door later and apologised, saying that she had been upset at a heartless hooligan entering our family.

"It's not my fault," I said, my resentment spilling out. "Why do you always use me as your punching bag?"

She didn't reply, but she cooked something nice that evening and I calmed down. During that hard time, food was another language in our home, often serving in place of words.

After their honeymoon, my brother went back to Sichuan and my sister-in-law moved into our house and later gave birth to my first nephew. Our two-year coexistence was never peaceful. She expected special treatment, not only as a pure proletarian who had "married down" to my brother, but also, paradoxically, for having produced the family's first grandson. My mother for her part, insisted that no uncultivated word or deed would be tolerated in her house. Whenever my sister-in-law passed on gossip, interrupted conversations, reached across the dinner table or sat slumped in front of guests, my mother would have a word with her afterwards. My mother never raised her voice, but I often heard my sister-in-law screaming: "Don't you dare use your bourgeois rules to control us proletarians! I'll write to my husband and tell him everything!"

I was unswervingly on my mother's side. I couldn't stand my sister-in-law, her greedy table manners, her messy bedroom, her rudeness to my mother. However, I didn't show her any hostility because my mother wouldn't allow it. "She's your older sister-in-law so you must show respect unless you want to become an ill-bred girl too."

During the Cultural Revolution, every residential compound had a leader and each street had a revolutionary committee. Apart from organising neighbourhood campaigns such as the digging of air-raid shelters and occasional night patrols, the committee had special powers to report class enemies to the police, to instruct Red Guards on which houses should be raided, and to recommend someone's deportation to the authorities. My mother was lucky that our compound leader was our front courtyard neighbour, a decent human being we children called Aunt Li.

Aunt Li had been unable to stand by and watch my sister-in-law's unruly behaviour and frequently helped my mother fight her. Once, Yang had become too friendly with a local Sichuan woman. When word of this reached my sister-in-law, she stormed into the yard, loudly cursing my mother for her son's "licentious behaviour". "This is no doubt the result of your bourgeois education."

My mother was outraged but would not utter a word, for she was too well bred to argue in public. Aunt Li had no such scruples so she shouted back: "Before you married Mrs Bi's son, he had done nothing wrong. What did you do to bring him down so low?"

One early winter's day in 1969, Aunt Li came into our house waving a letter at my mother. "What a rotten son you have! Have a look at this."

It was a letter from my oldest brother to the local revolutionary committee asking that my mother and I be deported to a remote region for reform. He cited his wife's report that my mother let me read *Dream of the Red Chamber*, a famous eighteenth-century novel that was currently banned, and expressed his concern that my young mind was being polluted.

Aunt Li burned the letter in our stove, cursed Yang and his wife, and told my mother to be on guard against my sister-in-law at all times.

After she left, my mother smoked a cigarette, then called me. "Let's go, let's send *his* wife and son away first." She took me to the household registration office of the local government and informed them that my brother had a permanent job in Sichuan and wanted his wife and son to go and live with him.

Years of revolution had plunged the country into economic crisis. People's daily needs were barely being met. However, the government always guaranteed supply for the capital because it was vital if they were to retain control over the nation that stability be maintained in Beijing. And so, nothing was valued more than a Beijing registration. As the head of our household, my mother had the right to do this on behalf of her son. As for the authorities, they welcomed anyone willing to surrender their Beijing registration and didn't bother to check with my brother.

Within half an hour, my mother had cancelled my sister-in-law and my nephew's Beijinger privileges, and destroyed my brother's only hope of eventually returning to Beijing.

I watched her calmly talking to the officers, occasionally laughing. She was a different person. Although I was happy to see my brother and his family properly punished, I was surprised by my mother's brutal actions. On the way back home, she stopped for a cigarette. Her hands were shaking so much that she couldn't strike the match. I offered to help and when I held the lit match up to her face, I saw a tear in her eye. Inhaling deeply, she said, "Do you know what it means to be deported to a remote village in this day and age?" She didn't wait for an answer but continued, "No one with a heart would do such a thing! But *my* son did – to his mother and little sister." She took another deep inhalation and said to me firmly, "Don't tell anyone about this. I can't afford to let people know I've brought up such a son. We can't bring trouble to your Aunt Li."

I nodded solemnly.

It was late at night when Yang came to collect his family the following month. My sister-in-law and her son were sleeping at the back of the house so my mother got up to open the door for him. She ignored his greeting and returned to bed. She never spoke to him again.

Now that my mother was dying, Yang was remorseful. He looked after her day and night and kept asking for forgiveness, but my mother would not meet his eyes. She did not forgive him. Shu, Ning, Dong and Jing all felt that my mother was too harsh, but I didn't. Yang had broken my mother's heart in the worst possible way. He had destroyed my mother's belief in herself. To me, it wasn't Yang she couldn't forgive, but herself!

I was quietly angry with my other brothers for what I saw as their unprincipled attitude. How could they expect my mother to forgive Yang after his betrayal? My question was answered more than four decades later. In 2014, when Shu, Dong, Jing and I met in Xi'an, I realised they knew nothing of Yang's letter, nor of Aunt Li's protection or my mother's retaliation. They had thought Yang was asking for forgiveness for his unruly wife. They were shocked, but since forty years had passed they immediately buried the whole affair and it was never raised with Yang. I was also shocked that my mother had never told them and at how such secrets could lurk in my family.

By the time my father was finally allowed to come home and see his dying wife, she had slipped into a coma.

Despite his tertiary education and his fabled erudition, my father was a traditional patriarch. Returning from his harsh labour camp, he wanted to enjoy some home comforts. My mother was dying and we were grief-stricken, but he focused on his own needs. "Has my tea been made?" "What am I going to have for dinner?" He was grieving, certainly, but his attitude seemed to be: "Since nothing can be done, what is all the fuss about?"

Indeed, my unconscious mother no longer needed care, but we were running around getting her grave clothes ready, informing relatives, fretting about the funeral expenses, and writing her a song – she had passed her passion for music on to her children.

We were stunned by our father's behaviour. We had thought that my mother had put up with so much in this marriage because of love, but where was his love? I was particularly resentful and avoided talking to him.

I was eight when my father left home for his desert exile. He only visited home a couple of times in the years he was away and he became a stranger to me. In the meantime, as I grew up I began to endure the financial struggles caused by his political problems and the harassment of his first wife, Old Mushroom. I was the sole witness to my mother's final years of misery – caused simply by having married him.

During one of his visits, he had given me a 20-fen note as pocket money. Instead of being grateful, I was angry. My mother had once begged me to go to a neighbour's house to borrow just such a sum because she did not have enough for my 1.25 yuan half-year school fees. Over the years I had also heard rumours from neighbours and from my mother's relatives that my father was tight with money because Old Mushroom was his priority. So I gave the 20 fen to my mother and stopped speaking to my father. On the day he was leaving, I did not say goodbye to him and left for school very early. My mother chased me half the way there. "Listen, we don't know when or if he'll be back again. How sad he would be if he didn't hear you say goodbye to him. What's wrong with you?" I followed her back but did not offer her any explanation. I said goodbye to my father only for my mother's sake.

On 24 October 1972, Uncle Yuji arrived very early. He had been at my mother's side every day since she had fallen into a coma. That morning he checked her and warned us it was a matter of an hour or two. Everyone got up and prepared themselves. His prediction was again correct. My mother died at ten o'clock, three days after my father had come home. My uncle and we six children were gathered around her when she left us; my father was sitting in the back room.

"I'm afraid to see a dead person," he confessed to my second-oldest brother when he went to fetch him.

Shu yelled, "That's not a dead person! She's your wife, our mother!"

This exchange left everyone except my uncle speechless. Uncle Yuji wept loudly over his "luckless" sister. Not brave enough to say it out loud, I confined myself to shouting at my father in my head, *When you're dead, don't expect to see me there.*

My parents were both highly educated. They had a high-class social life: they played bridge, recited poetry, knew some English and shared a love of Beijing opera and classical literature. Despite my father's selfish behaviour towards my mother, I know my parents loved each other. Two memories have stayed in my mind. The first was from the early days when my father was still in Beijing. One day after work, he asked me to go to Beihai Park to play with the other kids. For some reason I was back in a few minutes and saw my mother eating cake and my father making tea for her. By then my father's salary had been cut and we hadn't seen cake for years. My mother was embarrassed and annoyed when she saw me and said to him, "I told you this wouldn't do. She can smell cake from the other side of the world." To me, she said, "Come and help me finish this sweet thing. It's my birthday today." My father had wanted to do something special for my mother despite how dire their situation was.

Another memory was an exchange between my fourth-oldest brother, Dong, and my mother after a raid on our home by a group of Red Guards at the beginning of the Cultural Revolution. The Guards were probably from my father's company. Books were burned, floral patterned curtains torn, decorative objects – including toys – smashed, and drawers and wardrobes ransacked. When we were cleaning up after they went, Dong picked up a crushed model airplane he had spent a month building and spat out his resentment: "All of this is because of my father!" Jing and I were both home and we silently agreed. My mother stood tall and said to the three of us: "Your father has suffered much, much more. How sad he would be if he heard what you said." None of us responded but Dong stopped complaining and Jing and I worked harder to get the house back to normal. She had made us feel small.

Nevertheless, my parents were very different. My father was the youngest son of a rich landlord while my mother came from a long line of scholars. Her view of life was modern and Western while my father's was conservative and traditional. He believed men were the breadwinners and should be served by women. He didn't think there was anything wrong with having two wives, particularly since his marriage to my mother was partly a result of the war. "The Japanese were about to enter the town and your mother needed protection as a single woman," was his explanation to us and his argument to the court when he refused my mother's request for a divorce in 1957.

My mother had accepted the situation, comforted by the fact that Old Mushroom's status as first wife was an empty title. But not long after she returned from the hospital with her newborn daughter she learnt that, six months earlier and after eighteen years of separation, Old Mushroom had secretly given birth to my father's youngest son. This was the last straw and she took my father to court. After hearing my father's defence, the court threw her case out on the grounds that "the unfortunate entanglement was the legacy of the war. The three parties," it recommended, "should sort out their problems in a spirit of good will, especially for the sake of the two infants."

I had not known any of this until the late 1980s. I was doing a big spring-clean and found an old-fashioned briefcase. It contained the lawsuit documents and some letters of my parents. I didn't cry when my mother died, but when I read these papers and letters I sobbed uncontrollably, imagining from a mature woman's point of view the humiliation my mother must have endured: a modern and educated woman who had been forced to fight a concubine's war for the affections of a man. I finally understood why she had said I might have been a "bad omen": had I not been born, she might have been freed from this miserable triangle.

My mother withdrew her appeal against the court's judgment a year after it was handed down, because by then the Anti-Rightist Campaign had caught up with my father and with her. Their domestic struggle was set aside for the more urgent matter of survival.

After my mother's body was washed and dressed, I was asked to sit by her while everyone else went to the back room to discuss the funeral arrangements. I sat on a small bed across from her big bed, watching her and convincing myself that I could see her move. I had not quite grasped the concept of death. I was trying to talk to her, knowing I'd be seen as crazy, when something extraordinary happened. Old Mushroom walked in. My first instinct was to hide behind the bed, but she ignored me and went over to my mother. I was afraid she was about to assault her body, but she did not. She stood there, bowed tearfully to my mother three times and left.

I was frozen to the spot long after she left. And then I called Shu from the back room to tell him what had happened. He looked at me in disbelief and annoyance. "You know we're discussing serious things. Cut out your fantasy. You're too old for that."

"But she was here –"

"So what?" Shu said returning to the back room, shutting the door behind him.

I didn't tell anyone else because the mere mention of Old Mushroom upset my brothers. Many years later, my brothers accepted that she had come but nobody was interested in answering my question, "Why did she cry for our mother?"

Nearly twenty years later I found the answer. It was a windy spring evening in 1990, a month before I moved to Australia. Frail Old Mushroom knocked at my door. She had come to say goodbye. My cold reception didn't discourage her. She told me my mother was not a bad woman, but a loyal wife and good mother. She hated her for that, but respected her for the same reason.

I said nothing but my hatred began to give way to sympathy. As a traditional woman whose identity was bound up with her husband, it was only natural for Old Mushroom to do whatever she could to harm the woman who had stolen her husband. Looking after her man and her children was the main business of her kind. Her war against us was more a matter of survival than jealousy. Although my father was still providing for her at that time, I pressed a 10-yuan note into her hand when she left.

Then came my mother's funeral. In 1972, Chinese funerals were simple. For 28 yuan, a truck from the crematorium took the deceased away; for another 30, the body was cremated; and a pine box for the ashes could be had for between 10 and 50 yuan.

But we did not have this sort of money. Shu and Dong had scrounged around for every cent and borrowed heavily for Ning's and Jing's train tickets. Yang could not be counted on because his first priority was to buy something "important" in Beijing for his wife and son. My father said plainly that he had no money. So we had to turn to our uncle and aunts.

My mother had been an acclaimed calligrapher, a master of the Tang dynasty Yan style. Unfortunately, we children only saw her beautiful handwriting in the notes begging for a few yuan that we had all at one time or another taken to Uncle Yuji or Aunt Yuxian. We were so ashamed that we now had to beg for money for her funeral.

The discussion about the money, what for and how much, took place at Aunt Yuxian's home in Beijing. I was too young to be part of the meeting so I sat in the living room with my three cousins, my contemporaries. They didn't say a word to me, perhaps because they didn't know what to say, but I felt their cold contempt. Minute by minute I shrank further into myself.

The night before the funeral, the six of us children sat around our mother, singing a song written by Yang and Ning, the most musically talented of us. One line, "A family which has lost its mother cannot enjoy the warmth of spring again," felt to me like words of doom.

Following my mother's funeral there was a meeting from which I was excluded because it was about my future. It was disrupted by a terrible uproar. First Yang, Ning, then Dong dashed out of the back room, each of them in tears. Then Shu and Jing came out yelling, "Our mother is scarcely cold!"

My father appeared, red faced, and raised his voice: "She can't live by herself. This is the best solution." Then he turned to me. "Won't you want to have someone to cook for you and look after you?"

Shu answered for me, "Not Old Mushroom!"

They all stormed out. Before I could react, Aunt Li came in and took me to her house. "You must be very tired. Lie down on my bed for a while." She drew the curtain and closed the door behind her.

I hadn't cried at all when I was guarding my mother's body or at the funeral parlour when I watched the furnace swallow her casket, but in Aunt Li's dark room my tears welled up. I remembered my mother's prediction: "I'm afraid it won't be easy for you to walk away from Old Mushroom anymore." Memories of being attacked by my father's first wife haunted me. I cried myself into an exhausted sleep.

I wished Shu or Dong would talk to me but everyone was so busy over the next couple of days dealing with the cancellation of my mother's registration and preparing to leave that no one mentioned the issue again. And then one by one my brothers left. I didn't know what the future held for me but I didn't want to ask and expose my anxiety. I felt betrayed by my father and abandoned by my brothers.

My father stayed on. He had been granted this two-week break, and wanted to make the most of it. Every day I waited and waited for him to sit me down and tell me when Old Mushroom was going to move in. I didn't know how I would react, and I still don't know what I would have done. Very likely I would have accepted the reality forced upon me, just like my brothers had succumbed to the pressure of a ruling power. He was our father, after all.

Fortunately, Shu didn't stop fighting. A few days before my father's departure, I received a letter from Shu in which he said that if our father brought Old Mushroom home, it would destroy me, and our mother's worst fears would be realised. He would never let that happen. He would rather be called an unfilial son. If he had to, he would beat my father. The tone was alarming.

I am not sure whether I forgot to put the letter away or whether I deliberately left it open on the table, but I found my father reading it. He did not say a word, but the topic of Old Mushroom was quietly dropped.

On the day he left, my father handed me 30 yuan and told me that he had arranged with his company to continue to deliver this amount as my monthly living allowance. "Letting you, a fifteen-year-old girl, live by yourself is not my idea," he said. "From now on, you'll just have to make the best of it. You'll either survive or self-destruct."

Silence – my usual weapon for fighting against adults or the powerful – was my response to his intimidating remark. I wasn't scared, and I didn't think about being abandoned. I was just happy: what my mother feared most had been averted. I would not fall into Old Mushroom's hands.

3

The Will to Survive

The residents in our compound were a mixed bag. The thirty-three families included artists, diplomats, engineers, doctors, dentists, photographers, workers, teachers, a carpenter, a barber and a rickshaw puller. They had all moved in in 1951 when the compound became public property. Many years of cohabitation had made us an extended family. Adults looked on each other's children as their own, and youngsters called grown-ups uncle or aunt. Every festival – before the Cultural Revolution, that is – all the families would deliver good wishes and special delicacies to each other.

There were a few fruit trees in the compound: date, crab apple and apricot. Every autumn, the compound leader Aunt Li would organise a picking day and divide the fruit fairly between the households. This would be followed by a breakfast shared by the whole compound. A huge table would be set up in the outer yard, piled high with everybody's contributions of juices, jams, compotes and candied fruit ready to be enjoyed together. I can still see the bright display, the sunshine and the smiles on everyone's face.

When someone had a mishap, others would offer help without hesitation. Many years before my mother died, Aunt Duan was diagnosed with liver cancer and suffered dreadfully as her health declined. Aunt Li had drawn up a care roster for the entire compound to ensure that their neighbour Aunt Duan would never be alone. My mother often came home late with reports on how Aunt Duan was deteriorating.

All this changed after 1966. The Cultural Revolution made

everyone cautious and created distance between people. My father's political problem pushed people further away from us, and families like mine also kept their distance in case someone decided to harm them. People had become unpredictable.

So, after my mother died the neighbours didn't want to be involved in my family's affairs, whereas I was on my guard against the whole world, having experienced betrayal by my own father.

My brothers still call me cold-blooded, only partly in jest, because they had not seen me shed a single tear when my mother died. When they said goodbye my brothers' eyes were wet, but mine were dry. They didn't see me crying in Aunt Li's bed, didn't know how anxious I was about my future, and didn't understand that my faith in the people around me had been damaged. I had strong reasons for concealing my feelings. If my mother's own son could try to destroy her, and my father wanted to palm me off to Old Mushroom, what about the others? I was too young to see that it was largely the system, the abnormal circumstances, that forced them to behave that way, but I felt that by hiding my feelings and refusing help I would be less vulnerable.

The first "wind chill" of 1972 took place on 5 November, two days after my father left. The temperature dropped below zero overnight. It was normal for Beijingers to endure this kind of sudden change in early November, so households would spend a busy October getting ready for winter. There was no central heating in the traditional residential compounds. People had to move their stoves inside and install stovepipes as both smoke stacks and radiators to warm their houses. Ready-made quilts and quilt covers were unheard of back then so the sewn-on covers would have to be removed and washed and the cotton fill fluffed and topped up before being sewn together again, by hand.

Winter clothes, quilted cotton jackets and trousers, would also be remade in October. The lining and the fabric might be reused but the filling had to be new cotton for warmth. One more task was buying cabbages. Since fresh vegetables were not available during winter, the government gave every Beijinger a special ration of 40 kilos of cabbage days before the first "wind chill." These cabbages were carted home and carefully stored or pickled so they would last for three months.

But that year, none of this had been done in our house. In early September, my mother had briefly contemplated doing my winter clothes. She had taken them out of the trunk one day and put them back the next. She probably did not want to accept her approaching death, or perhaps she simply did not have the strength to do it. My mother had taught me how to clean the house, wash underwear and socks, sew hems on garments and make basic meals. She had not trained me in the routines of preparing for winter, because these were adult responsibilities. Aunt Li ordered her husband, a quiet handyman, to install the stovepipes for me but I had to deal with the rest.

My first task was to get sixty cabbages home from the co-op. When I handed over the ration coupon and paid for them, the woman in charge asked me: "Where are the adults in your family? Go call them to take the cabbages home." At first, she refused to believe that I had no adults to call on, but after deciding that I was telling the truth, she offered to help load me up with cabbages. They had been lying in a corner of the co-op for several days and were covered with a thin layer of ice. I could only carry four half-frozen cabbages at a time, so I made fifteen trips to the co-op and each time she would stop whatever she was doing and come to help me.

After she had loaded the last cabbage, she thrust a small paper bag into my pocket. Inside were broken bits of sweet pastry – the sort of freebies that co-op sales assistants were given. "Something sweet for you, you deserve it," she said. Such kindness from a total stranger reduced me to tears.

I had seen how the neighbours did it, so when I got the last cabbages home I stacked them neatly on the veranda against our front bedroom window, covered them with a thick layer of straw to keep them from freezing, and secured this with a couple of bricks. My arms were sore for days, but I enjoyed the sweet taste of the pastry and my little triumph in getting the cabbages home.

My second task was washing the bedding. Our family had five quilts of wadded cotton and after our chaotic October they were dirty and smelly. There was no washing machine, no washing powder and no hot water so I removed the covers and soaked them in a big washing tub. I sat on a small stool with half a bar of rationed soap and washed the sheets and covers on a ribbed hardwood washboard. I started in the morning and didn't finish rinsing the last sheet until past midnight.

My fingers were swollen and the skin on my palms was peeling, but that was not the end of it. I had to wring out the wet sheets and quilt covers by hand – a job my mother had often asked my brothers to do. They would each hold one end of a big sheet and twist it into a thick rope until all the water was squeezed out and then open the sheet out and shake it violently to smooth it out before hanging it on the line. I was on my own and lacked my brothers' strength so the bedding was still dripping wet when I hung it on the line. Watching the puddles form on the ground, I was so disappointed with myself that I seized the sheets from the bottom, wound them around my body and twirled around several times in a bid to squeeze more water out. My clothes were soaked and the sheets continued dripping. I cursed my brothers as dirty pigs and myself as hopeless.

The next morning, the overnight sub-zero temperature had frozen the sheets and quilt covers into hard boards with icicles. Worried about the neighbours' criticism, I tried to take them off the line before anyone saw them. All this left me with was scratches on my hands and face and one broken quilt cover; it simply snapped in two. I ran home empty handed, threw myself on the bed and cried because I had made a very expensive mistake. It was not just the cost of replacing the cover, it was also that cloth coupons were limited.

Utterly defeated and exhausted, I fell asleep and didn't wake up until the afternoon. I remembered the sheets and quilts on the line and rushed out. I was so happy to see that the warmth of the sun had restored them to soft fabric.

I spent the rest of the afternoon and that night sewing everything together. Sewing the covers back onto the cotton quilt was hard. The needle had to be thick and long in order to go through layers of material. The old cotton fills were tough. I put my mother's thimble on my ring finger but it was too big and kept falling off. By the time I finished sewing, there were pricks all over my fingers.

The following day Aunt Li came to see how I was going and saw my damaged hands. She took me to her place, applied ointment to my broken palm and carrot-like fingers and then wrapped them in gauze. "Are you really a mute mule? Can't you ask me? Or anyone? Who wouldn't give you a hand? Your mother will curse us in heaven." She wiped away her tears even as she scolded me, but I just stood there silently, biting my lip and holding back my tears. Inside, a voice said, *I don't need a hand from anyone!*

From that day on Aunt Li called me "the girl with a stone heart". I didn't defend myself. In fact, I was happy to be so regarded since I didn't want others to know how I felt.

I did not dare remake my winter garments, although over the previous year I had grown a lot and my old jacket and trousers were short and tight. I just wasn't up to the job. Mrs Han had a sewing machine and offered to help me remake my winter clothes but I declined. She worked six days a week as a tailor in a factory, and had six children to look after. Her sewing machine was going almost every night from after dinner until very late. But my refusal was not out of consideration for her. Any help I accepted would register as evidence of my failure to live independently. I didn't want the option of living with Old Mushroom to resurface.

Another ordeal I faced was keeping the indoor stove lit. The government had recommended honeycomb briquettes as the most efficient fuel. In summer, each house was allowed up to six briquettes per day for cooking and in winter this was increased to ten to allow for heating as well. Every month we were also given five combustible briquettes for lighting the stove. This was enough for most families because people were too poor to consume more than their ration. But that was not the case for me that winter.

The key to using a stove efficiently was knowing when and how to operate the stovepipe lock, which controlled the airflow. The coal would burn quickly when the stovepipe was fully open but when it was locked one briquette could last for eight hours; this was called banking up the fire. My stove frequently died from either over-burning or over-banking. Before the end of the first week, I had used up all five of my igniters, leaving me only one way to re-light the stove – exchanging briquettes with neighbours. I would exchange one of my new briquettes for a half-burned one to rekindle the fire.

Some neighbours would make sure their half-burned briquettes were in the best condition to guarantee my stove would spring back to life; others would exchange one nearly burnt-out briquette for a new briquette of mine and not worry whether my stove would revive or not. So my coal ration was consumed quickly and well before the end of the month when new briquettes were supplied. I was forced to eat cold leftovers, and cover myself with the four remaining quilts to withstand the night chills. Some nights, I got up and did the aerobics that I'd been taught at school to try to warm myself up. I was miserable, not because of the discomfort, but from feeling defeated and having allowed myself to be cheated by those greedy neighbours.

I was always cold that first winter. I had frostbite on my feet and exposed ankles (from my short trousers) and my hands were chapped. My mother had played piano in her early life and had often said that my long slender fingers would have been wonderful for playing piano. I look at them today, long, perhaps, but definitely not slender. A legacy of that cold winter.

My ultimate challenge was organising the monthly 30-yuan stipend. On the first day of each month, a Mr Liu would cycle round to deliver it. He was around fifty, tall, thin and soft-spoken. Every time he passed me the envelope with the money in it, he would say the same thing, "Look after it and make it last till my next visit." Aunt Li was in charge of the ration coupons. Every month when she gave me the coupons for flour, rice, cooking oil, eggs, meat, tofu and so on, she would also remind me to, "Look after it and make it last till the end of the month."

Rationing had started in the 1950s, initially with grains, cooking oils, and fabrics. With the breakdown of production during the Cultural Revolution, it was extended to most daily needs, including matches, soap and toilet paper. I had a monthly ration of 13.5 kg for "staples" consisting of flour, rice and cornmeal. "Non-staples" were eggs, 1 kg per household per month; cooking oil 250 mL per person; and tofu 200 g. Meat was not rationed for it was too expensive to enjoy often anyway. Nor were green vegetables rationed because they were too scarce.

I had witnessed my mother's struggle to make ends meet, so I knew a little of how she managed things. But I was only a child and for years I had had no pocket money. When I used to go out with friends or classmates, I had been the only one who didn't buy a snack. It was not just me who felt awkward in those situations, my companions did too. They didn't like eating their treat in front of me, knowing that I couldn't afford one. How I had wanted to buy a snack together with my friends, not only to satisfy my gluttonous cravings, but also to raise my standing among them. I especially fancied two things – fried pancakes and Friendship Brioche. Now that I controlled my money, these desires became irresistible.

Early morning on every street corner in Beijing, there would be two big pots set on two massive stoves with a bench beside them. One pot was filled with oil and the other with soya milk. A male chef would knead dough with oil, alum and salt, roll it into small pancakes, cut two slits in each one, and deep fry them. A female assistant would take the customers' money, ladle the hot soymilk into their takeaway containers then fish a pancake out of the oil, wrap it in paper and give it to the customer. People would queue up to buy for the whole family. They were cheap enough that most families could enjoy this traditional breakfast once or twice a week, but I had not had any since I was ten.

Friendship Brioche was a fashionable picnic food for students. This French-style raisin bread had been introduced by the Vietnamese government as a symbol of friendship and was stocked in every co-op. Since Year 6, I had been going on numerous school excursions – protesting all day in front of the embassy of the Soviet Union, marching half the night in celebration of Chairman Mao's latest supreme instructions, or dancing for hours to welcome foreign guests such as the Sri Lankan prime minister, Mrs Bandaranaike – and my classmates would feast on a Friendship Brioche with an apple while I ate a cold steamed bun with a cucumber.

I had been contemplating these purchases since my father handed over the 30 yuan the day he left. The completion of so many hard tasks in my first week alone was partly motivated by the pancake and brioche I had promised myself. So one morning, I got up early and queued for my first reward – the pancake. No words can describe my excitement as I watched my pancake float in the oil and inflate as it turned golden and then finally took my first bite. That same day, in the afternoon, I bought a brioche for dinner.

I had planned that I would buy one pancake a week and one brioche a month. But I kept finding excuses to buy more. On 25 November, I had no money or food coupons left and all my grain bags were empty.

I tried to solve the problem calmly because my mother had told me many times that panic brought not help but disaster. "When an unfortunate thing happens, nothing can send it back. You have to face it with a cool head and a practical attitude." I comforted myself with one of her stories of how she went without food for three days in a bunker during a Japanese bombing attack. She had said, "As long as you have water to drink, you'll be fine."

I scooped up the last handful of rice, shook out the flour bags thoroughly and made a big pot of porridge. It was water-thin, but I believed it was nutritious. My mother had told me another story when she was persuading me to drink rice soup. A loving son instructed his wife before he left home to take up his appointment, "I'm the only son so please look after my mother carefully." When he returned six months later, his mother was lean and haggard while his wife was glowing with health. Furious, he sued for divorce. In tears before the judge, the wife cried: "I'm wrongly accused. I always scooped up the rice for my mother-in-law and I only had the leftover liquid."

All the nutrition, my mother had explained, was in the liquid. If she could survive three days on just plain water, I should be fine for five days with rice water. I would get the new monthly allowance on 1 December.

But I was not fine, especially at night. I was so cold I could not fall asleep. When I sat up, I felt dizzy and nauseous. By the evening of 28 November I was lying in bed feeling I was about to die. I worried about the neighbours discovering my dead body. They would tell my family that I had not been able to survive on my own. My second-oldest brother would scold me for letting down the whole family, my mother in particular. I tried to stop crying by telling myself that the dead heard nothing, I would not hear his harsh voice, but then the thought that I could be dead got me going again. I had to do something instead of waiting to die.

I got out of bed and made two decisions. The first was to bring in a cabbage after all the neighbours went to bed. I had fed chickens chopped raw cabbage when I was little and I reasoned that since I was born in the year of the rooster, it might be okay for me too. The second was to use the chamber pot instead of going outside to the toilet when anyone else was up and about. *Mustn't let anyone see me looking sick.*

But I did not end up eating chicken food. When I was in the toilet at midnight emptying my chamber pot, I met another teenager who lived in the house opposite and whose name was Third Daughter.

One of the old beliefs in Chinese culture is that "good names bring the evil eye". If parents give their children an eye-catching name – like Rich Luck for a son or Golden Bird for a daughter – they might attract bad luck. So some traditional families give their children plain names, such as Small Nail for a worker's son, Zucchini Flower for a farmer's daughter, or simply numbers to ward off the evil eye.

Third Daughter was another "orphan" in our yard. Her mother had died long ago, leaving her and her older sister, Second Daughter, to be raised by their father, Mr Tong.

Mr Tong had never been employed by the Communist government so he stayed home during the day. Children liked him because he often helped us cover up our mistakes before our parents returned home from work. For example, he often cleaned up my bloodied knees after Old Mushroom attacked me and promised me he wouldn't tell my mother.

One hot day in 1968, a black jeep had stopped outside our gate. Two plainclothes policemen walked in, and asked where the Tongs lived. Schools were closed at that time and all the kids were in the outer yard playing ball games. I was among them and we led the policemen to the house. We watched as Uncle Tong, in a white T-shirt with a little hole in one shoulder, gathered up some clothes and put them in a black imitation leather bag then ask permission to go to the toilet. One of the policeman drew a handgun and followed him to the male toilet and then to the jeep. His daughters watched with us. Not a single word was exchanged between father and daughters and no one asked any questions or made any comment.

I was shocked by the revelation that kind Uncle Tong was a hidden enemy, and went to ask my mother if she was surprised. "No," she replied, "nowadays, anyone can be an enemy. Your father is one, so don't gloat about it." I felt her disapproval.

No one saw Mr Tong again. Five years later, in 1973, the girls were called to attend their "seriously ill" father in prison. They returned home wearing black armbands. Mr Tong had been dead when they got there. "My father's body was completely black," Second Daughter told the neighbours. During the Cultural Revolution, many, like Mr Tong, died without explanation.

After their father's arrest, Mr Tong's two daughters became famous in the compound for their "ill-bred" nature. They fought with almost every neighbour over anything, no matter how trivial. My mother had warned me never to get involved with the sisters. "They're wild and they'll bully you."

In 1969, Second Daughter had been sent to the far northeast to be re-educated. Third Daughter had a deformed leg so she was given a job in a neighbourhood factory making matchboxes.

Third Daughter was two years older than me, but once she joined the work force, she dressed and behaved like an adult. That midnight in the toilet block she looked at me and asked, "How long since you've had something to eat?"

Frightened of the consequences, I refused to answer.

"You can't lie to me," she said and took me over to her home.

I forgot my mother's warning and followed her. I desperately needed help.

Without saying a word, she poured hot water for me to wash my face and soak my feet and prepared a small bowl of vermicelli soup for me.

I was grateful but suspicious at the same time. "Why are you so kind to me?" I broke the silence.

"Because I have had a taste of starvation."

There was very little soup so I finished it in no time. She took the bowl away and explained, "I'm not being mean. When you haven't eaten for a long time, your stomach can't handle too much food. I learnt this from *painful* experience." Then she opened a drawer and handed me a 5-yuan note and some food coupons. "Remember, this is *once only*. I won't help you again because it's bad for you." She was very serious. "You're a good student so you can figure it out. After you've paid me back, you will have less of your next monthly allowance left. If you don't do something about it, you'll start borrowing more and will never be able to catch up. Then you'll become a real skunk. Please, don't let them laugh at us."

She did not explain who the "them" were and I did not think to ask.

I even forgot to thank her before going back home. That she had saved me was unexpected, and the way she had dealt with me – as one of her circle – was surprising. I had hardly talked to her because my mother had made me believe that she and I were different. She had no respect for elders while I never talked back to anyone older than me. But now Third Daughter was helping me. Her "once only" advice was particularly touching because I was intelligent enough to know how right it was.

But I did not dwell on this because I fell asleep straight away. Warmth and sleepiness came with a full tummy.

In December, I did not buy a single pancake or brioche and watched my expenses carefully. On the last day of 1972, Mr Liu delivered my January money a day early. I was excited because I still had a twenty-fen note and 250 g worth of food coupons left. I reported my success to Third Daughter on New Year's Eve.

She was in a bad mood but I was too excited to notice the tears in her eyes until she said, "So what? It's no good." Staring at my stunned face, her tone became sharper: "How far can twenty fen take you? You're lucky this Mr Liu came a day early. He might have decided to come after the two-day New Year break. Then what would you have done? Why are you so hopeless?"

My mother's warning immediately came back to me. She had helped me so she felt entitled to bully me! I fought back, "I've paid you back and won't borrow anything from you ever again," and I walked away, enraged.

She called after me but I ran faster; in the end, she followed me home. My stove was dead again, but I was used to the cold and also wanted to preserve my last ignition briquette for New Year's day. She saw this and went back to get a burned briquette to rekindle the stove.

She explained why she was so angry. One of her stovepipes was rusted through. She had found it that morning and knew she had to do something about it because it could cause carbon monoxide poisoning. "You know how much it would cost?" She answered her own question with a face full of pain, "Three yuan!" She began to cry. "I have been saving for my leg operation. I don't want to be a cripple forever. Now a pile of money has gone just like that."

She had inquired at the hospital and found that the operation would cost 330 yuan. She had saved up 175 yuan and now she was back down to 172. "I wanted to have my leg done before my nineteenth birthday. The doctor said that I need six months to let the bones grow together and another three or four months before I can walk properly. My dream is to walk normally by the time I'm twenty."

The concept of saving money amazed me. In my short life, making ends meet had been the whole purpose of life. Now I wanted to be like her and save money for a dream too!

We talked a long time that New Year's Eve – or rather, I listened to her. She told me that learning to cook well was the best way to save money; imagining unexpected misfortune at any moment was another strategy because if you had put the money away and the unexpected did not happen, the money would already be saved. She also told me her proper name was Min, meaning smart. "But my kind of smartness is only useful for housewives. You're the real smarty. Don't waste it on daily trivia!"

Once more she surprised me. She had a far clearer view of herself than I did of myself. I had preferred to be alone since my mother died as it made me feel safe. Now I was glad to have a friend who was more experienced at surviving on her own and survived well!

In January, the windows in my front room often misted up inside, sign of a warm room in winter. I learnt to place my shoes next to the stove at night to have them dry and warm the next day. I cut the damaged quilt cover into four pieces and sewed the pieces onto the tops of the other four quilts. In this way, I did not have to wash the whole quilt cover often since the top of a quilt was the dirtiest part. I had imitated Third Daughter successfully in many ways, except for cooking.

The most common staple food for Beijingers was steamed buns. They were filling and required neither oil nor condiments. But making them required skill, starting with the dough. There was no such thing as self-raising flour so you had to leaven the dough and leave it to rise beside the warm stove for hours. Then came the tricky part. You had to soak some baking soda – it was rationed – in a bowl of boiled water and when it cooled add it to the dough and knead it through. You had to achieve the right density and an even distribution of the soda water in order to balance out the sour taste. All of this was too complicated for me. My dough usually turned out either sour or bitter. I did not like the sour taste and often used too much soda which turned the buns olive green. I was known in the compound as the green-bun eater.

Winter was cabbage-eating season for northerners. No other vegetables were available until Chinese New Year, when the special festival supply kicked in. To make cabbage more appealing, people chopped it finely, mixed in spices and an egg or fifty grams of fatty mince and wrapped the mixture inside dough that they would steam or panfry. The chopping was time consuming, the skill for making the mix was daunting so I decided to consume the cabbage in my easy way, by boiling it in big chunks and mixing in a bit of salt.

My first three months of independent life consisted of one lost battle after another. But I had made gains in one respect – I learnt to see people as they really were. My mother was choosy about who she socialised with. Of the thirty-three families in our compound, she associated only with the educated and well-mannered. Aunt Li, who talked loudly, ate noisily, and moved clumsily, was too rough for her. For a similar reason, I had been forbidden to befriend Third Daughter. But during those difficult winter months, it was these two who demonstrated kindness and generosity. Aunt Li would scold me roundly but at the same time provide me with the best burning briquettes to revive my stove, the best leavening to make steamed buns, and a bowl of anything special she cooked for her family.

While Third Daughter treating me well was a case of like attracting like, Aunt Li's actions came from a fundamental decency that can easily disappear in adverse circumstances when everyone is struggling. Some of my mother's well-mannered friends were only interested in "helping" me use up my rations of eggs, tofu, or vermicelli or, worse, treating me with contempt.

One of my most hurtful moments came courtesy of one of those neighbours. It was after my three days of starvation during which they had probably seen me out (at the toilet) secretly at midnight. It was common knowledge that I could not make my briquettes last so these particular neighbours suspected I was up to theft, and ordered their children to keep an eye on me. For days, whenever I went out, whether to pour dirty water down the drain or go to the toilet, this neighbour's door would open and a head would pop out. I had cheerfully greeted the different heads until their youngest son said to me innocently, "Do you have to come out so often during the night? I'm cold but my father wants me to watch you."

I questioned him in an equally innocent way: "Why do you need to watch me?"

"You're so poor you might steal from us."

"Steal what?"

"Cabbages or briquettes." He was dragged in from behind and must have been slapped because I heard him crying.

My mother had raised me with the highest moral standards to be hardworking, self-disciplined, respectful and honest. Now here I was being regarded as a potential thief. It was unbearable.

I had only cried twice since living alone, once over my quilt cover and again over the likely outcome of starvation. I had been too preoccupied with survival to mourn the loss of my mother, but that night I missed her terribly because if she had been with me I wouldn't have suffered such an insult.

The next day the neighbour came to apologise for his son's "mad idea and silly behaviour". He was visibly relieved when I seemed to be agreeable, and once again he asked if he could help me use up my rations. I politely refused his request. "Sorry, I've used them all up," I lied shamelessly. Watching his retreating back, I savoured my victory.

I had gained the wisdom of judging people by their actions not their words but I also learnt to lie.

4
Winning Respect

Before he left Beijing, my father had arranged with my school that, to preserve my academic record, I would be allowed to skip the mid-semester exams at the end of November 1972 and return to school afterwards.

But he hadn't consulted me. Despite having missed all the classes, I still wanted to sit the exam. Perhaps this had to do with my fear of being bullied again by Ling: the poor result I was bound to get would please her. Or perhaps it was just defiance. Having made my decision, I returned to school on 13 November for revision week.

Everyone had learnt of my mother's death, and my teacher and classmates, including Ling, felt sorry for me. Not knowing what to say, they were tiptoeing around me. I sat at the back of the classroom beside a very shy new girl and took advantage of being left alone to take in the teacher's instructions fully.

That was the week after I had completed my difficult tasks at home and was gorging myself on pancakes and brioche. My house was clean so my mind was sharp; my tummy was full, so my body could withstand the cold. Every day, I revised the lessons and prepared till midnight or even later since there were no adults to hustle me off to bed. Most of what I had missed was memory work, which was not a problem for me. But I had missed quadratic equations in mathematics, which demanded plenty of practice. Parts of it were challenging but I did not want to ask anyone for help. In fact, I did everything I could to conceal my efforts from my teachers and classmates. I had to prove that I could be fine on my own in every way, and it was the sweetest sensation ever when I solved an equation.

The exam timetable was cruel, with six exams over three consecutive days. Chinese language and literature was always first, followed by politics, history, geography, science and foreign languages (English or Russian). Maths was last, on a Saturday afternoon (until 1995 Saturday was a normal school day). I felt frustrated after the maths exam because I had left some questions unanswered, and I returned home to face my three days of starvation.

By the following Tuesday, my teachers and my classmates noticed how dejected I looked and assumed I must be upset about doing badly in the exams. Our form teacher called me into her office during lunch break and comforted me with Chairman Mao's words: "What's most important is one's attitude, not the result." In the afternoon in front of the whole class she praised my bravery and urged me to face any disappointing exam marks with the same spirit.

My classmates took this opportunity to break their silence, echoing the teacher's words to show their kindness. Even Ling turned around in her seat to give me a smile. How could they know that I was not upset, just hungry. I was too hungry to be moved and show my gratitude. Only when the new girl, who was too shy to even speak, simply gave me a piece of leftover pancake from her lunch did I smile at her with a tear in my eye.

Wednesday afternoon the form teacher chased after me as I walked out of school. She had just seen my marks and was excited. "You'll know by tomorrow and everyone else will too, you have nothing to worry about! You did so well, it's amazing!"

By then I had received Third Daughter's loan and I was thinking clearly again. The teacher's reassurance made me very anxious. I spent the night worrying about the reaction of the others, particularly Ling. They might decide my downcast look early in the week had been a manipulative attempt to win sympathy or, worse, a sinister plan to make everyone else look foolish. I could not defend myself because I didn't want anyone to know that I had been starving. That would prove I was incapable of living on my own. For the same reason, I had to hide the fact that I was now surviving on a loan.

I went to see Third Daughter for advice. She said, "I told you last time, don't let them laugh at you. I tell you now, don't let them crush you either. You don't need to argue or fight with them. Just believe you're stronger than them."

"Who's them? My classmates? How do you know them?"

"You're so silly!" Third Daughter said. "Anyone who looks at me or you and sees an orphan, an easy target, that's who 'them' is!"

Suddenly I saw the light. We orphans had to look out for ourselves if we were to survive and win respect. I said to myself: *Be strong. You earned your results.*

But I did not face any animosity the next day. When all the marks were added up, I had come top again, though by only a tiny margin. The immediate reaction of my classmates was disbelief. Then there was a round of applause, led by Ling! Once more I was surprised. I had thought that no one would care whether I won or lost, especially Ling.

Ling became my strongest supporter from that moment. She regarded me as a disadvantaged girl with a defiant spirit like hers. Grateful though I was for her support, I couldn't forget how she enjoyed wielding power. Nor could I forget that she was the confident child of a revolutionary family, while I was the offspring of a Rightist and an active reactionary.

In 1972 academic achievement was appreciated once more so I became popular. During the breaks and after school, I often found myself surrounded by my classmates. The smart ones would discuss the hard questions with me and the confused ask for my help. I felt encouraged and was happy to hang around with them now. I was willing to answer their questions because I wanted to repay them. Like any teenager, it felt good to belong.

Our lunch break included the midday nap; in winter, the break was two hours and in summer, three. Most students went home to eat with their families and have a nap afterwards, but I usually stayed at school. After having lunch at the school canteen, I would sit in our empty classroom and help someone either complete their homework or prepare for a test. Sometimes I would stay after school till late as well, since I had no parents waiting for me to get home on time.

My form teacher became worried. She knew that I had been bullied before so she was concerned that I was being exploited now. She called me into her office again.

"No one has the right to stop you having a proper break or going home after school. Just say 'no' to them!" she told me loudly and angrily.

I was alarmed because my form teacher was always smiling and rarely raised her voice. But seeing her take off her glasses to wipe her eyes made me realise she was protecting me, like a mother, from being taken advantage of. Hesitantly, I assured her that I was doing the work voluntarily. She resumed her form teacher's role: "Ah, that's good. If you're happy to help others, that's a different matter. As Chairman Mao says, 'We should help one another and care about one another'."

Helping my classmates actually benefitted me. Firstly, it meant I spent less time at home feeling cold and alone. There was a huge stove in the middle of our classroom and the maintenance staff kept it well stoked. Secondly, I was eating better. Although I could only afford a bowl of rice with a complimentary soup at the school canteen, it was warm and well cooked. And from time to time I found a meatball or a piece of egg at the bottom of my soup, "accidentally" dropped in by the canteen staff – they too had learnt of my mother's death. These pleasant surprises made me smile and somewhat restored my faith in people.

Above all, I was pleased to discover that I could explain things well. My early school reports had consistently contained comments such as "highly intelligent but extremely shy" or "lacks communication and social skills". These comments were devastating because from a very early age I had dreamed of being a teacher.

When I was five, my mother had dragged me to the neighbourhood kindergarten. I put up a big struggle, kicking and screaming all the way. At the front door of the kindergarten, my exhausted mother let go of me and, as I lay on the floor screaming, told the principal teacher to forget about enrolling me. The teacher ignored her, leaned down to me and said, "I'll take you home after I show you something. Come, come in with me." Her voice was soft but authoritative, and the way she looked at me won my trust. I stopped crying, got up and went inside. For years afterwards my mother raved about this teacher and the magic she worked with children. That incident inspired my dream of being a teacher.

When I was in high school, there was much talk about "future careers". I had told my mother that I wanted to be a teacher and she had shared this knowledge with her sister, my Aunt Yuxian, who was a teacher herself. Aunt Yuxian pooh-poohed the idea to my face, saying that I did not have the right personality for it. This happened during one of our visits to borrow money. Although my mother was fifteen years older than Aunt Yuxian, she always appeared less opinionated than her younger sister and she responded softly, "It's her dream. What can I do about it? Let's see."

On our way home, I held my mother's hand and felt closer to her. I had interpreted her response as a vote of confidence in me. She was clearly pleased that I had understood and had given my hand a tight squeeze. I felt a connection with her at that moment. Nevertheless, my aunt's comments had effectively shot down my teaching aspirations.

In my second year of high school, my desire to teach was rekindled by our new literature teacher, Mr Wang.

For the entire first year of high school, I found literature lessons boring because everything had been weeded out of our syllabus except a few masterpieces of classical prose and some short stories by early twentieth-century pro-Communist writers. My classmates felt the same way and our literature lessons were often the rowdiest. We had to find ways to amuse ourselves. One day, our young literature teacher taught us emotive set phrases. When he explained the phrase 痛不欲生 (be so grief-stricken as to wish one were dead), one boy stood up, assumed a pitiable look, opened the window, and jumped out. Our classroom was on the top floor of a three-storey building so the teacher panicked, "Help! Help! He'll be killed!" What he didn't know was that the drop outside that window was barely a couple of metres. The poor teacher was about to have a heart attack when the boy walked back in and asked if his understanding of the phrase was accurate. The class erupted in laughter, and by the time we quietened down, my stomach ached from giggling.

But Mr Wang always had us under control, not by yelling but with his literary insights and his ability to foster understanding, along with his subtle but powerful way of guiding us through the stories. He was quiet and spare with words so I began to fantasise that a "mute mule" like me might yet be a teacher.

Many of my classmates had told me that my explanations were clear and easy to follow. At first I thought they were just being kind, but in January, when the top students formed a peer tutoring group with the aim of achieving a "failure-less class", I was the tutor most in demand. This encouragement undoubtedly fostered my future obsessions with storytelling and teaching. The efforts of our tutoring group generated a great interest in learning and I became a popular student not only among my peers but also with the school authorities.

At the beginning of the Cultural Revolution, Chairman Mao had instructed school students to question everything they were taught and to be alert to their teachers' ulterior motives. As a result, many teachers had been brutally attacked and some even murdered. This violence had stopped by 1972 but the confrontational attitude to teachers persisted.

Our class was the top academic class in the school, but we also had a reputation for being the most undisciplined. We would argue with a literature teacher about her choice of a descriptive word, a maths teacher about his way of reaching a solution, or a history teacher about her interpretation of an event. We were very close because most of us had been classmates since grade one. If one student had trouble with a teacher, we would all be there to back him or her. However, the new interest in learning shifted our energy from finding clever ways to harass teachers towards discussing intelligent questions with them. Our school was very pleased with the change.

Despite my popularity, I did not drop my guard one bit. I would not approach anyone to offer help, nor would I volunteer suggestions. Even when others asked for help, I would allow them to decide where, when, and how we would do it. I declined most invitations to join group activities. I was fully aware of my "bad origins" and knew my place. I filled in my spare time with housework and challenging maths or physics. I learnt to enjoy isolation and felt safe in it.

Very soon this self-awareness proved necessary. When our class needed to select someone to be in charge of academic study, I was elected unanimously, but in the end it was Ling who was chosen by the school. Everyone was disappointed, and Ling was upset. She refused to take the position and accused the school of deliberately setting her up as "an enemy of the people".

I was not happy but it did not surprise me in the least. It was not the first time that my "bad origins" had limited my participation in school activities. Ever since primary school, I had missed opportunities such as enrolling in elite schools, joining the literacy or maths competitions, and going to summer camps despite my brilliant academic record. The most recent case had taken place just a year before.

Late in 1971, China had decided to open up to the world. The government invited many foreign guests to Beijing and set up grand receiving ceremonies. If the guest was the head of a country, there would be a hundred thousand people lining the Boulevard of Eternal Peace to welcome them as they stood with Premier Zhou Enlai in an open car. The welcomers would wear the colourful traditional costumes provided by the government, hold paper flowers or balloons and shout the guest's name as they danced.

Because our school was located near Tiananmen Square, it had been selected twice, once to welcome Emperor Haile Selassie from Ethiopia and once to welcome Prime Minister Sirimavo Bandaranaike from Sri Lanka. The entire school had trained every afternoon for two weeks for Emperor Selassie's visit in October 1971. All of us, the girls especially, were terribly excited, but on the very last day as we were trying on our costumes, three students were summoned to the principal: Li, an epileptic; Hua, who had enunciation problems; and me. We were told to stay behind.

The principal felt sorry for me, a top student with no physical impediment, but as this was the first important national diplomatic event in this new era, anyone from a family with "current" political problems had to be excluded. Since my father had mangled Chairman Mao's "Never forget class struggle" into "Never remember class struggle", his daughter would likely pose a danger to the national interest.

I told the principal that for the sake of my beloved country, I would fully comply with the authority's decision. This was not a lie. I had been trained to believe in the government's policies. But later, at home, I repeated my words in tears to my mother.

However, I did participate in the welcome ceremony for Mrs Bandaranaike eight months later in July 1972. Due to the need for masses of students, my school had decided to let Li join the team, but she had a seizure a few hours before the event. Our school's task was to hold paper flowers as we formed the word "welcome" in front of Tiananmen Square. One missing person meant a black hole in the word. Desperate, the form teacher came to fetch Hua, who was sitting with me in the empty classroom watched over by a maintenance worker. When Hua learnt the news, she shed tears of joy. But her joy was short-lived because she could not properly pronounce the guest's name, "Bandaranaike". After half an hour of this, the form teacher gave up and went to see the principal, who made the bold decision to let me fill that last blank place.

In a normal society, I should have felt absolutely humiliated but I cannot say that that was the case. The memory of how the ceremony went has left me but I do recall afterwards excitedly telling my mother how close I had been to Premier Zhou Enlai and what heavy make-up Mrs Bandaranaike had been wearing. It wasn't that I was too young to feel humiliation, but rather that I regarded this kind of discrimination as inevitable. It was my role to be a child of "bad origins" under the proletarian dictatorship.

Expecting disappointment has almost become my default attitude, an attitude formed when I was growing up in Mao's China. Healthy and natural it may not have been, but it helped me cope with adversity. In the winter of 1972, armed with this outlook, I was not crushed by the overturning of my election as class representative. Ling was finally persuaded to take the position, and she became even nicer to me. In the meantime, I carried on my tutoring and received the most pleasant of surprises: books.

Books were absolute rarities at that time. Indeed, the suppression of literature in Communist China had started in 1942 with Mao declaring that writers had to place themselves at the service of the revolution. From that point on, Chinese literature was limited to depicting class struggle. It was mainly classics of Russian literature, along with a few works of O. Henry and Charles Dickens that were translated in the 1950s and '60s, for they could be fitted into the framework of social realism. Even so, before 1966 there had been books to read. During the ten years of the Cultural Revolution there was a total ban on arts and literature, and by early 1973, all that remained were two novels, *The Golden Boulevard* and *The Female Island Militia*. The rest were "poisonous weeds". Reading them was illegal.

But there were plenty of "poisonous weeds" in the homes of powerful people. The rationale was that these people had made a great contribution to the Communist cause, and their class consciousness was so high that they could withstand the poison.

At that time, all students attended local schools since the selective high school system had been abolished. In our neighbourhood there was an important military compound accommodating senior cadres. Quite a few of our classmates were the children of generals or colonels. They usually struggled at school because their education had frequently been interrupted when their parents kept being transferred.

And yet their elite families had high expectations for them. Under such pressure, they often turned to me for help.

One was the son of a super-strict lieutenant-general who would belt him if he failed to get good marks, so he was a regular client of mine. One Saturday afternoon, he asked me to stay back after the bell.

"Didn't we finish your homework yesterday?" I asked.

"Well, there's one question I have to ask you." Checking that no one was around, he fetched a big book out of his school bag. "Would you like to read this book? It's very good, famous too. It's because I want to thank you. But you have to promise not to tell anyone and to bring it back on Monday morning or my dad will kill me."

The big book was Victor Hugo's *Les Misérables*. The image on the cover, the pen-and-ink drawing of little Cosette holding a mop and bucket, has been engraved in my memory since the moment I saw it. I hardly slept that weekend and finished reading it just before school on Monday morning. It was a sketchy reading. Hugo's insights into education and literature and his social and theological concerns were wasted on me. I only followed the storylines to find out the fate of Jean Valjean and Cosette. However, some details I remembered vividly – the food on the table of the bishop's home: soup, bacon, mutton, figs, fresh cheese, a large loaf of rye bread and a bottle of his old Mauves wine. I found it odd that a meal like this should be regarded as "ordinary fare" – what about my cold cornmeal bun?

My classmate was relieved that I returned his father's book on time. He mentioned he had more like that at home so I promised to do my best to help him get good results at the end of the semester if he could keep providing me with books to read.

I had been using my knowledge to gain benefits such as a share of my classmates' lunchboxes, but my conscious bartering started with this agreement that Monday.

*

I had grown up with books and stories. Back when we still lived together, my parents' room was crammed with books. Our birthday gifts were always books. When I was five, they bought me a picture book about a little boy with a magic pen. Everything he drew with it would come alive. I liked best the image of a colourful rooster that flew off the wall. Jing, my fifth-oldest brother, had also read the book and was crazy about a sailing boat that began to ride the wind and cleave the waves as soon as the boy added the last stroke to his drawing. The two of us began to cover every wall of the house with drawings of roosters and boats, but none of them came to life, and our furious mother made us scrub the walls clean.

My parents liked to share what they read with us. My father was good at telling stories, especially of legendary historical figures and events. Before his political problems escalated he spent a lot of time with me, teaching me to read and write and telling me stories. He had also regularly taken me to a small storytelling theatre in the West-Single-Archway Department Store, where I enjoyed watching the storytellers on the stage waving fans and making the audience laugh or weep.

Another teller of stories was our nanny, an older woman from my father's village who we called Fourth Grandma. She had been the concubine of one of my father's brothers. During the land reform of 1948, when land was seized from landlords and redistributed among poor peasants, this brother and his family had been executed by the Communists. His concubine had been spared because of her poor family origins and lowly status. She found refuge in Beijing with our family and worked as a live-in nanny from 1952 to 1957. After my father's fall, she worked for other people to help my parents survive the crisis. In 1966, my mother sent Fourth Grandma back to the village, both to shield her from any harm caused by our family's problems and to avoid any problems her history might cause us. While my father had led me into Chinese history and literature through his written stories, Fourth Grandma dazzled me with her countless folk tales. As a child, I would fall asleep each night listening to the telling of a story, either by my father or by Fourth Grandma.

My mother had held onto a few classical novels such as *Dream of the Red Chamber* and *Journey to the West*, the story of the Monkey King, until the end of the 1960s with the excuse that these books were national treasures. When my brother Yang's girlfriend first visited our house, she brought fruit for my mother and a picture book for me. I was nine years old and, to show off, I brought down a thick volume of *Dream of the Red Chamber* and told her that *that* was my normal reading. Insulted, my future sister-in-law turned her anger on my mother: "You'll do anything to humiliate me, a daughter of the proletariat." Surprisingly, my mother didn't blame me for causing trouble for her at that moment. Soon after this proletarian young woman married my brother and moved in, though, she burned those books.

But the lack of books did not put an end to the storytelling in our house. During the years when it was just me and my mother living in the house, she read a huge dictionary, which, because it was a reference book, was not targeted by the Red Guards. There are many four-character phrases in Chinese that are literary or historical allusions and the dictionary gave the origin of these expressions. For example, there was the expression "fictitious land of peace", against which newspapers were then warning people. There was no such place, the editorials said, because everyone had to participate in the revolution and class struggle. My mother told me the original story of the "fictitious land of peace" had been written by Tao Yuanming, a fourth-century poet who lived through the chaos of war during the East Jin dynasty:

"A fisherman lost his way home and walked into a village on the other side of the mountains, where people knew nothing of politics and struggle. They lived in peace and prosperity and could not understand the turmoil the fisherman spoke about."

My mother paused, and asked me, "Would you like to visit this village?"

"Yes," I replied excitedly.

She sighed and told me the end of the story: "Although the fisherman marked the trail back to the village, neither he nor anyone else could ever find it again."

As she read on, she explained other allusions: about the frog at the bottom of a well who believed that heaven was a round hole; the person of the state of Zheng who failed to buy himself a pair of shoes because he had left the measurements at home; the thief who covered his ears while stealing a loud bell but managed to wake the guard; and the turtle who preferred freedom in the filthy mud to adoration inside a palace cage. I learnt so much about Chinese culture and literature as a result of my mother's perusal of the dictionary that it was no accident that I studied and later pursued an academic career in literature and philosophy.

After my mother's death, more books came from the son of the lieutenant-general and from other classmates in the same military compound. I was delighted, yet worried. Reading banned books was a crime punishable by public denunciation or by detention. I had to read in secret. I was fearful, but I couldn't resist the urge to know those wonderful stories. I reasoned: *those generals can read these books because they have made a contribution to the country. I have helped their children so I have earned my right to read them too.* Unfortunately, that rationale did not convince even myself. I decided to take practical measures – I bought curtains for the front rooms.

Our house had an elaborate façade because it was the master house in the compound. Entry into the house was through a pair of tall French doors. Flanking the doors were large glass windows across the entire six-metre frontage. The whole design proclaimed extravagance and beauty, but not privacy. We once had fine curtains to protect our privacy, but they were torn down by the Red Guards at the beginning of the Cultural Revolution because of their "bourgeois" floral pattern. New curtains were now necessary to hide my secret reading.

By the end of January 1973 my domestic life was under control and I had saved 3 yuan. February was a short month so I made the first big purchase of my life, spending nearly 6 yuan on curtains for the living room and my bedroom.

Spending such a large amount of money was exciting but also nerve-wracking. I carefully measured every window and every pane in our front door and did my calculations countless times before buying and cutting the fabric. I chose a thick cotton with dark red stripes of different shades. It seemed to fit the purpose – when I pinned them up and looked in from the outside with the lights on, I could see nothing. But I had not realised that you need to allow two and a half times the width of the space for curtain material. After two nights of sewing, I was shocked to see that there were gaps on both sides of my meticulously measured curtains. I had to stretch the fabric across the gaps and thumbtack it in place.

This was indeed a setback but such a setback could by no means overpower my joy in reading those marvellous books. Night after night, I absorbed the words of Austen, Hawthorne, Hugo, Dickens, Stendhal, Tolstoy, the Brontë sisters and other classic writers. Since my suppliers often attached unreasonable time limits to returning the books, I sacrificed many hours of sleep, sitting on a small stool, positioned next to the stove, reading through the long winter nights.

My life as an orphan took a positive turn when I returned to school. I was no longer lonely, and I won respect. I was being stimulated by the knowledge I was acquiring and the enthralling books I was reading. I also learnt to reflect: when Ling and other classmates had stopped socialising with me before my mother's death, I had felt ostracised, but now I liked to keep my distance. I enjoyed the company of my classmates yet was happiest on my own. My conclusion: life seemed easier if one could live it fully, without needing the help, company, or approval of others.

5

Food and Dignity

The approach of Chinese New Year's Eve on 2 February 1973, a week-long celebration that revolved around food, reminded me that my cooking skills were in great need of help. Although this would be my first New Year without my mother, my focus was solely on my discomfort in the kitchen rather than on missing her.

After my return to school I had been buying lunch at the school canteen and regarded this as my main meal of the day. Dinner had been make-do: usually a cold leftover bun with pickles or, if the stove was alive, a bowl of soup – a bunch of dried noodles or a cup of rice thrown into boiling water with salt and chopped cabbage leaves for flavour. Not at all satisfying.

I rarely accepted neighbours' offers of food except for the occasional bowl of leftovers from Aunt Li or Third Daughter because I trusted them. I would wolf down the warm food they offered me. Aunt Li would always say to me, "Slow down! Don't act like you've never tasted good food, knowing the family you come from!" But these two were the poorest neighbours and their food was the most ordinary.

Indeed, at one time no family in our yard ate better than mine. While others focused on meals that were warm and filling, ours were gourmet tastes.

My father was a connoisseur when it came to food. He was from a village in Henan province which, he said, possessed a secret recipe that had been famous since the Song dynasty, twelve hundred years ago. Called the "Three-Eights Banquet", its eight cold dishes, eight hot dishes and eight desserts had graced weddings, funerals and celebrations in the region for generations. In his village, my father claimed, the first criterion of a prospective wife was how good a cook she was, from daily snacks to banquets. When the matchmaker had presented his prospective wife, Old Mushroom, to my father's parents, my grandfather doubted that a girl from a wealthy landlord family would be able to cook and knocked back the proposal, but Old Mushroom was stubborn. She had the matchmaker deliver to my grandfather a basket of steamed buns, a sheet of handmade uncooked noodles and a container of finely shredded carrot salad.

The buns were as white and shining as babies' faces, the noodles fine as hair, and the shredded carrots like long, soft thread. Every time my father mentioned this – which was quite often – my mother would storm out of the house, bringing Father's reminiscences to an end. Initially, I enjoyed hearing him talk about those fine foods but then I felt guilty for showing interest in his story when I saw how my mother reacted. His praise of Old Mushroom was an insult to my mother, so I too walked away when my father began to talk in this vein. Years later, I wondered if my father had never been able to make a clean break with Old Mushroom because of my mother's lack of interest or expertise in the kitchen.

Although my mother believed that a woman must be independent and self-sufficient, and educated me accordingly, she was never much of a cook. For most of her life, she had no need to be. Born into a bourgeois family, married to a high-achieving engineer, and a career woman herself, she had always had helpers in her house. I always admired the 1950s photograph of her that was in our living room. In it, she looked anything but a housewife: she was wearing a fashionable jacket, double-buttoned with a slim waistline and big folded collars, and her long hair was stylishly permed. This life of hers had not helped her become a good cook, but it had acquainted her with good food. From an early age, my brothers and I learnt about many famous Chinese dishes from our parents' dinner-table talk: Beijing roast duck, Shandong smoked chicken, Shanghai stir-fry soft-shell crab, Sichuan chilli fish, and so on.

We also had Fourth Grandma living with us, and she could turn ordinary ingredients into mouth-watering dishes. For example, during the famine years of the early 1960s, cornmeal became the staple food. While the children of other families moaned about eating rough and dry steamed corn bread and pickled radish day after day, from time to time we could feast on her crispy corn pancakes, stuffed with fine shredded radish, cabbage and clear noodles, mixed with salt, pepper, a tiny bit of chilli and a few drops of sesame oil.

Fourth Grandma's skills really shone during the New Year celebrations when there were good ingredients to cook with. In the old days in a typical Beijing residential compound, New Year feasts were an undeclared competition. Fourth Grandma would spend days and nights preparing exquisite dishes. As a child, I took all of this for granted and was only interested in the snacks she made for us – deep-fried gold and silver butterfly-shaped dim sums, crunchy shallot rings, crystalline frozen gravy, and twisted osmanthus biscuits – and so I have forgotten many of her true masterpieces.

After my father was labelled a Rightist and had his salary halved, Fourth Grandma went to work for other families in the neighbourhood to help our family out with money. So my mother, having been forced to quit work, had to take on cooking for the family. What a shock that was! To our refined palates, it was like moving from a Michelin-starred restaurant to a canteen. Whenever Fourth Grandma snatched a little time from her other work and returned home to cook for us, I felt that we were celebrating a festival.

Nonetheless, my mother never failed to put a warm meal on the table, especially in the last few months of her life. She had learnt to make steamed buns, crispy pancakes, noodles with tasty sauces and many stir-fried dishes. She even learnt to make some poor people's dishes – from the outer leaves of cabbage or ageing vegetables – things she would normally have thrown in the bin.

Two such dishes often found their way to our table: dried eggplant pickles and steamed celery leaves in a dough mix. Overripe eggplants, full of seeds and inedible, were sold for next to nothing. My mother would bring a bundle home, slice them thinly at different angles to make them coil, salt them thoroughly, then hang them from a rope to dry. Then she would shake the seeds off and steam one or two with garlic as a dish. This dish cost very little, used no oil and gave us a bit of variety.

Celery leaves were considered too bitter to eat, but my mother would wash them well, mix them with flour and salt, and steam them. A few drops of sesame oil on both dishes made them more appealing.

There were two enamel food containers in our family's kitchen cabinet. The thick base of these containers was designed to keep cooked dishes warm and fresh for a long time. One of my happiest memories is coming home from school at lunchtime to see the containers on the stove waiting for me. If I didn't see them on the stove I would call out, "Where's my lunch?! I'm hungry!" After my mother died, the two containers were kept inside the cabinet and were hardly touched. Whenever I saw them, I missed the food my mother had cooked that seemed very appealing.

Chinese New Year was the festival of food. The number one delicacy was dumplings, because it was the tradition to eat dumplings when the midnight bell rang. The Chinese word for dumplings, 饺子 (jiaozi), is pronounced the same as the word for a smooth passage from the old year to the new, 交子 (jiaozi). Dumplings were also the biggest sore point in my independent life.

None of my neighbours had ever offered me dumplings because they were not daily fare. Dumplings were small so the filling had to be fine and sticky. To achieve this, it was essential to have more meat, eggs and oil. In other words, they were expensive to make. During the last years of my mother's life we could only afford dumplings on Chinese New Year's Eve. The image of steaming hot roly-poly dumplings being dropped onto my plate along with my mother's command – “Eat them while they’re hot” – has stayed with me.

I had made one attempt at dumplings back in early January but it had been a total disaster and had completely cured me of any ambition to become a cook.

It was 5 January 1973, Xiaohan 小寒, the day of the Little Cold, which marked the advent of winter’s coldest days. Traditionally, every household was supposed to eat dumplings to show their readiness for the coming long winter. After school, I joined the queue in the co-op and bought fifty grams of mince. Returning home, I brought a cabbage inside, chopped it finely, mixed it with shallots, ginger and the mince, and began to make dumplings.

I did not know how much filling I should prepare for one person. I had also failed to squeeze the chopped cabbage dry. I kept rolling out wrapper after wrapper and in the end I made more than a hundred dumplings, most of them not properly sealed because of the watery filling. When I boiled them, the filling leaked into the water and they ended up shapeless and tasteless.

I ate the terrible dumplings for breakfast, lunch and dinner for two days until I was really sick of them. I wanted to throw the rest in the toilet, not the one in our yard but the one outside on the street. During that tightly rationed period, waste was a crime and anyone who wasted “staple food” could be labelled as sabotaging the revolution. I wrapped the leftovers in newspaper, hid them behind a trunk under the bed and decided to wait until nightfall when no one was around to take them out. But by night-time I had forgotten all about them. When a strange smell appeared a week later, first in my bedroom and then right through the house, I washed everything but the smell only got worse. Finally, I cleaned the house from top to bottom and it was then that I discovered the paper parcel, green with mildew. Cursing myself for being so useless, I threw the parcel into the public toilet out in the street after midnight.

I had been aching to eat dumplings to the point of losing my dignity. The evening after I realised that my new curtains did not cover the windows, I went to ask Third Daughter for help. As soon as I entered her house, I was overwhelmed by the smell of meat, fresh chives (part of the New Year's special ration), ginger, shallot and sesame oil. She was making dumplings! Her sister, Second Daughter, was back from her re-education site in the far northeast and together they were making a special dinner of welcome.

Third Daughter stopped the dumpling making and came over to see if anything could be done about my curtains. It was her idea to use thumbtacks to stretch the material. I thanked her and she left. Instead of feeling happy that my problem was solved, I was upset because I had been hoping to be invited to taste her dumplings. I tried to focus on my reading but failed. Half an hour later, I was at her door again, this time without a pretext. She was just scooping the cooked dumplings out of the pot while her sister was setting the table.

Third Daughter hesitated but then invited me in. From her reaction I knew I should leave straight away, but I didn't. She asked her sister to put another plate out. Second Daughter did so, placing it on the table with a loud thump. My face was burning with shame, but I simply took the plate and ate the five dumplings on it. Quietly uttering some words of thanks, I left. On my way out, I heard Second Daughter say, "A beggar! Her mother would have died of shame." I ran back home, disgusted with myself.

Years earlier – I would have been about four or five at the time – my third-oldest brother, Ning, had been reprimanded for stealing a meatball from the canteen counter at school without paying for it. My mother had been so ashamed that she had gathered Ning, Dong, Jing and me together and given us a lecture. I was very alarmed at how angry she looked and ended up sobbing loudly. After she had calmed down a little, she told us a story from the Chinese philosopher Mencius, about a dying beggar who refused food because it had been given to him with contempt. "That's called dignity. The beggar had a backbone. Without a backbone, life is worthless," she said.

I had lost my backbone over five dumplings. What would my mother have said, knowing her daughter had become a "beggar"? And what would my father, Old Mushroom, and my brothers think? I could not sleep, going over and over these questions. The darker the night grew, the more distressed I became.

In those days, public denunciation was routine. Prearranged or spontaneous, on-the-spot denunciations would take place in a residential compound, at school, on a bus, almost anywhere. Every week at school assembly at least one student would be denounced for either fighting in public or flirting with a member of the opposite sex. The unfortunate targets would be encircled by the whole school and their wrongdoings exposed and criticised. Seeing the unlucky ones shamed filled us all with fear.

My imagination ran wild in the dark of the night. I saw Second Daughter standing in the middle of the yard, loudly broadcasting my shameless behaviour even as she humiliated my dead mother. I saw myself standing in the school grounds being vilified for wheedling treats out of the canteen staff and my classmates. I saw the angry face of my second-oldest brother as he screamed, "You let our mother down!" Of course he would be angry. He had risked being seen as an unloving son so that I wouldn't fall into Old Mushroom's hands. And I saw Old Mushroom holding the 30 yuan that should have been my allowance as she ordered me to move into her house or, worse, as she moved into our home and my mother's room. I saw myself being abused by Old Mushroom's younger son, my half-brother, just like Jane Eyre was by her cousin John in the book I'd been reading that day. A sense of doom overwhelmed me, and I lay in bed sweating and shivering.

Looking back, I probably suffered a panic attack that night. But in those days in China, nobody knew or cared about mental health. My lifelong insomnia and nightmares started that night, as did my paranoid initial reaction to any unpleasantness in my life.

With the light of day my wild imaginings retreated and my mother's advice came back to me: "When an unfortunate thing happens, nothing can undo it. You have to face it with a cool head and a practical attitude." I got up with a decision to atone for my behaviour by buying the two sisters two fried pancakes with a pot of hot soy milk. This cost much more than their five dumplings would have cost, but it was necessary. I had to do something to forestall the ghastly consequences I had imagined; I had to put up a fight.

This decision sprang from another of my mother's dictionary stories, "Fold One's Hands and Await Destruction", about a battle that took place during the Three Kingdoms period (220–65 CE). The inhabitants of a besieged city were facing slaughter. Their leader asked them: "Should we simply fold our hands in our laps and await destruction? Or should we put up a fight?" Everybody, soldiers and civilians alike, put up such a ferocious and spirited fight that they overwhelmed the enemy and the city was relieved. My mother had commented at the end: "You know what? This kind of resistance still often ends in destruction, but if you fight, at least you have a chance of winning."

When I presented the pancakes and soy milk to the stunned Second Daughter and heard her murmur, "Oh, there's no need, you're too generous," I knew that doom had been averted. I had gained the upper hand and was safe.

Back home, instead of pleasure I felt only disgrace and falsehood because I had achieved the upper hand through bribery. I gazed up at my mother's photo and swore I'd learn to cook and never again lose face for the sake of good food. My spirits lifted after this declaration and I was able to hold my head up the next time I faced Second Daughter.

To my delight, my fourth-oldest brother, Dong, returned home to celebrate New Year with me. To welcome him, I had made an effort to clean the house and stock up on supplies for the festival.

Giving the house a good clean on New Year's Eve is a tradition going back thousands of years. It is meant to stop any bad luck the family has from continuing into the future. Although not a traditional woman, my mother observed this old custom religiously, perhaps because our household had had more than its share of bad luck. While Fourth Grandma and Dong would be preparing the feast, my mother would lead our cleaning team. Windows and doors were opened for hours to let any bad air out; ceilings and walls were dusted, book shelves wiped, floors mopped, bedding changed and the water pot filled to the brim. When everything was done, we were ordered to wash and change into new (or clean) clothes. Celebrating Chinese New Year in a spotless house was a family ritual.

When he arrived, Dong was very happy to see the house clean and me surviving well. I was happy too, not just for his company or the chance of being looked after for a few days, but because Dong was an excellent cook who would be able to give me cooking lessons during his break and, in particular, teach me how to make dumplings.

My mother had often praised Dong as "every parent's dream child": good-looking, intelligent, considerate and diligent. When I was little, Dong had been my favourite brother. He had often given me gifts – a colourful ribbon, a shiny hair-pin, a bead bracelet – and he had taught me calligraphy and drawing, and helped me win second prize in our primary school art competition. Fourth Grandma also loved him because from a young age he had been a great help to her. Dong never left the kitchen when she was preparing the New Year feasts. He was the only person in our family who could serve the Three-Eights Banquet. He even bested Fourth Grandma by learning other regional cuisines. Our father would sometimes take Dong along when he went to a restaurant. Dong would examine the various dishes, their look, smell and taste. Afterwards, if we had the ingredients, he would reproduce them in our kitchen.

In March 1969, when Jing and six other teenage neighbours were sent to the far northeast or southwest to be re-educated, our compound leader Aunt Li (two of whose daughters were among the group) suggested the families involved pool some money for a farewell banquet for the "poor kids". Dong was appointed chef and cooked for more than thirty people. Everyone said that the food was better than in the restaurants. In later years, Dong was often called upon to produce family banquets for weddings, birth ceremonies or funerals.

My cooking lessons with Dong started with making dough.

Chinese dough is just flour and water – no salt, butter, eggs or any extras – so it is much harder to make the perfect dough for different purposes. Noodles need stiff dough, pancakes soft dough, dumplings neither stiff nor soft. Other recipes require steamed dough or baked dough, unleavened dough or leavened dough. In addition, the water temperature, the kneading method and the right length of time for the dough to develop tenacity and elasticity are all crucial.

Dong explained that well-made dough should be smooth and shiny, and so should the dough maker's hands and utensils. He was a patient teacher, and I was a determined student. During his two-week holiday he taught me to make steamed buns, white, shiny and sweet; noodles, thin, tough and long; and pancakes, crispy on the outside but soft and moist inside.

Dong only made dumplings once on New Year's Eve. In addition to mince, eggs, cabbage, chives, shallots and ginger – the usual mix everybody used – he added a handful of small dried shrimps. When the New Year firecrackers began to explode outside, Dong took the cooked dumplings out of the pot and put them on our plates – twenty each! We ate them slowly in order to savour the divine taste fully. Dong was in tears. When I asked why, he said evasively, "The dumplings are too hot."

I woke up in the night hearing Dong sobbing in the back room. When I went in, he told me that he missed our mother. I felt bad because I didn't. I wished that I could cry with him but my eyes were dry. While Dong was caught up in his grief, I was totally absorbed in dumplings. For Dong, the pain over our mother's loss was still raw after three months. But I, preoccupied with survival since day one, had had no chance to process my grief. Dong finally fell asleep but I stayed awake till dawn. I began to believe that I was truly a cold, unfeeling person. It worried me then and has ever since.

Dong did not teach me how to make dumplings. "It's too expensive. For a big family it may be affordable but it's too much for one or two people." Seeing my disappointment, he said, "I can teach you lots of cheap dishes that are easy to make and delicious."

So I learnt to make steamed lazy dragons and its finer versions: butterflies or twisters. I flattened the leavened dough, spread the mixture on it – similar to the one for dumplings but much rougher – rolled it up into a roll as thick as my arm and steamed it. Then I cut it into many pieces so I could eat it over several days. Or I cut the cylinder into pieces before steaming them and pressed down in the middle of each piece with a chopstick so that both open sides turned up and it looked like a butterfly. I then twisted the butterfly into a lovely twister. This recipe combined the staple and non-staple foods most economically.

I ate well during that New Year period and felt contented. It gave me a great feeling of pride and achievement when I delivered my steamed butterflies or twisters to Aunt Li and Third Daughter. I was finally interacting with my neighbours as an equal. To add to my delight, my February expenses came in well below budget.

From that New Year on, I began to pay attention to good food, as my parents had. Even in the books I read, any description of food would attract my special interest. One of my classmates lent me Guy de Maupassant's *Collected Short Stories* for the New Year break. His "Ball of Fat" made the most vivid impression on me because of the account of the food the protagonist shared with her fellow passengers in the fleeing carriage: roasted chicken on a bed of its own jelly, pâtés, fruits, sweetmeats and wine. I dreamed that one day I would be able to sample those exotic dishes and develop tastes as particular as my mother's, who said it was better to eat a single mouthful of fresh peach than devour a basketful of old apricots.

6

Stories, Music and Imagination

By the spring of 1973, my house was in order and I was managing to save a small amount each month. When my brothers learnt that I had become a good housekeeper, they started inviting friends who were visiting Beijing to spend a night or two in our house. This was their way of forming *guanxi* (good connections) with colleagues. Our double-sized back room, with its back entrance, was perfect for putting guests up.

I would often find some stranger waiting at the door when I got home. They would show me my brother's signed note, and I would let them in. I didn't mind. At the time, staying in a hotel was an alien concept as people could not afford it and they usually stayed with friends or colleagues. For me, having visitors from time to time was fun. It added interest to my solitary life. It was also no trouble because, as a minor, I was usually not expected to offer any other hospitality than a bed.

Once, though, my second-oldest brother, Shu, invited his best friend's son to stay in our house for the night. In his note, Shu asked me to cook dinner for this guest, a young man barely twenty, because Shu and his wife had dined at his parents' home in Xi'an. It was the last day of March, and I had just proudly put my month's savings into my new bank account and had only one egg, one tomato, and one bowl of rice left for my last meal of the month. Mr Li was due to deliver my April payment the next morning.

I cooked the rice and a small dish of egg and tomato for the guest.

"What about you?" He looked at the table, set for only one person.

"I had my dinner at school. I'm sorry it's so simple."

One of my mother's strict social rules was to never embarrass your guests so I watched him wolf down *my* dinner with a smile on my face and hunger pangs in my belly.

In his job as a purchasing agent for the turbine factory in Sichuan my oldest brother, Yang, travelled everywhere in search of timber, steel and machinery, and wagons for transporting the goods back. He and his fellow agents had built up a network of free accommodation to save on their travel allowances. He invited many agents to our house.

Goods shortages and the woeful transport system made purchasing agents' jobs so difficult that they were usually inflicted on persons of "bad origins" like my brother. In most cases these people were from intellectual families, well-educated and all great talkers. They had to be, to persuade suppliers to sell them goods, and dispatchers to assign them rail wagons. As thanks for putting them up, these purchasing agents told me stories of their travels. I learnt a lot about remote regions, about the customs of minorities, the wildness of the provinces, and the delicacies of the Sichuan basin. I was fascinated.

One day Little Zhang turned up. He was a bookish young man who did not talk much but when he looked through my bookcase he discovered my secret stash – Alexandre Dumas the younger's *The Lady of the Camellias*, a thin book wedged between two huge volumes of Marx's *Das Kapital*. I was worried that he would report me to the authorities or even to my oldest brother, who had disowned our mother for the sake of the revolution. Worst of all, how could I face my classmate if this book he had lent me was confiscated?

To my surprise and relief, Little Zhang flipped through it, put it back then asked if I knew the author's father had written a more famous book, *The Count of Monte Cristo*. When I shook my head, he said it was the most brilliant of stories. "Do you want to hear it?"

Do I? I thought as I looked at him. I was not sure if he was testing me – wanting to listen to a poisonous story would reveal one's bourgeois class standing – until I saw the eagerness in his eyes. "Of course!" I nodded excitedly.

Zhang was an excellent storyteller. He sat in a big chair facing the door. "If you're a good storyteller, your listeners will be all ears and won't notice anything. I'll sit here just in case anyone walks in." Sitting quite upright and looking straight ahead, he recounted that riveting tale of revenge. His eyes sparkled behind round glasses and his voice was sometimes soft and sometimes so powerful that I would gasp. He started telling the story after dinner and continued late into the night. It was a long story, and he was tired after nearly forty hours on the train from Sichuan to Beijing, so he went to bed at midnight, before Dantès had even escaped from the Château d'If. The next morning, he left before I was up. I was miserable because I desperately want to know Dantés' fate, and I knew I might never see Zhang again.

Most visitors stayed only one night because there were restrictions on out-of-town visitors staying in Beijing's domestic households unless they were family members or had exceptional reasons.

At school, I asked my book lenders if they had come across *The Count of Monte Cristo*. No one had. Back home, I remained miserable until after dinner I picked up *The Lady of the Camellias* where I had left off earlier and became absorbed in the tragic love story. I had just settled down when there was a knock on the door. Zhang was back!

"There's no meeting tonight so I've come to finish the story. I thought you might want to know what happened."

I was overjoyed. I thought he was the most considerate person in the world. I did not realise that his urge to share a riveting story was perhaps even stronger than my desire to hear it.

Aunt Li always kept an eye on me. She was angry with my brothers, and particularly my oldest brother, for letting strangers stay in my house. "Irresponsible! Selfish! Has he thought about you at all?" she would curse when a guest left and while she was doing the "check-out" inspection.

Sometimes, as soon as someone turned up she would come to investigate, firing questions and scrutinising their official references and the note the guest had brought. I often felt she belittled me in front of the guests. Once I even complained to Third Daughter about her nosiness and the two of us had a nice rant together. Now I see clearly that she was worried about me and protected me. How lucky I was in those years to have a neighbour like her!

That night, Aunt Li noticed that Zhang had come back. Just as he was picking up from where he had left off the night before, she walked in and asked why he was still there. Zhang stood up respectfully and explained that he had already checked into his guesthouse but was back to finish a story.

"What story?"

"A story about capitalist society, how dark and unfair it is," Little Zhang replied. He sounded confident but looked tense.

"That sounds good. We must criticise capitalist society ruthlessly." Aunt Li seemed satisfied with Little Zhang's summary of the story.

I relaxed, admiring Zhang's shrewdness. But Aunt Li didn't leave. She turned to me and surprised me by asking, "Is it a good story?" Without waiting for an answer, she turned back to Zhang: "Can I bring my little one? He loves stories, and we haven't had any for a long time."

Beijing's traditional dwellings were built around a courtyard. Weather permitting, neighbours would sit in the yard under the trees after dinner and chat about all kinds of things: books, movies, plays and domestic trivia. Beijingers have long been famous for their eloquence and passion for storytelling. But in 1973 there were no books to read, and virtually nothing to see in the cinemas or theatres. People's revolutionary alertness was so high that daily trivia could easily be construed as counter-revolutionary and used to turn someone in. Everyone was bored so anything different that also fitted in with revolutionary values, such as criticising the darkness and unfairness of capitalist society, was appealing.

With Aunt Li's endorsement and her son for company, over the next few evenings I listened to *The Count of Monte Cristo* right to the end.

Zhang left Beijing, but the storytelling in my house did not stop. First, Aunt Li's son asked me to fill him in on the part of Dantès' story that he had missed. And then he wanted me to go over the whole thing again, "Please, because I hadn't heard the first part, I was confused in many places. The foreign names were so hard to remember. You have a good memory so please tell the whole story again. It's really good!" I didn't want to waste such a wonderful long story on him alone so I called Third Daughter and she brought along another neighbour's son. More and more youngsters came. Every time a new listener joined in, I had to go back over what had gone before.

To keep the story fresh for the earlier arrivals, I became creative. Zhang had skipped lots of details since he was pressed for time, so I filled these details in. I described the ship Dantés sailed on by drawing on my fifth-oldest brother's drawings of ships. I evoked the bullfight by adapting the description of the fights between lions and gladiators in Italian author Giovanni Orie's *Spartacus,* which I had just read. For the tastes and smells of meals in the novel I drew on my newly acquired culinary skills and my imagination.

One of my new listeners was the boy who had been ordered to spy on me that winter's evening after my mother's death to see if I was a thief. I still nursed a grudge, so I was prickly with him. Others could be late, but he could not; others could make comments, but none of his comments were tolerated. He was a keen listener and obeyed whatever rule I imposed on him. However, he would sometimes become so absorbed that he forgot himself. When anything exciting or horrifying was about to happen, he would inject sound effects into my narration.

There were two old feature films showing in 1973, *Landmine Warfare* and *Tunnel Warfare*, both about resisting the Japanese invasion. Whenever Japanese soldiers appeared, there would be two beats – *den den* – that got louder and louder as the films went on. This boy must have watched those films once too often so that when things got going in the story, he would insert a *den den.* At first he kept his voice down, but as he got carried away his *den dens* became so loud and frequent that they broke my rhythm. I was annoyed and so was my audience. I ordered him to leave.

He left, but with tears in his eyes. Half an hour later when I went out to the toilet, I saw him sitting outside my door trying to eavesdrop the rest of the story. The spring nights were still cold, so he was shivering. I felt sorry but didn't want him to feel I had forgiven him for once having taken me to be a thief.

"Why don't you go home? Do you want to get sick?" I asked in a stern voice.

"I don't want to go home. I want to listen to the story and your story is so good. I promise not to make any more noises. I'll seal my mouth with sticky tape. And," he stood up and whispered, "I'll let you listen to my father's records. They're bad bourgeois records, but they're very beautiful. Please, don't tell anyone."

I allowed him to return to the storytelling circle. My grudge was nothing compared to the temptation of listening to his father's banned records. His pleading had also appealed to my vanity as a storyteller.

The boy's father had been a rich businessman in Shanghai before the Communist takeover. He had a turntable and a few dozen records hidden away at the bottom of an old wardrobe in their corner storeroom, but his children had discovered them and secretly listened to the records when their parents were at work. So I had music in my life again, but it was very different from the music I had grown up with.

We were a musical family and loved to sing – mainly contemporary Chinese or Russian songs. They were usually about the prosperity of our great motherland, and the melodies were cheerful and uplifting. However, by 1973 even these songs had long been forbidden because any melody pleasing to the ear was labelled "decadent". What we sang every day were songs eulogising Chairman Mao –

> Heaven is vast and earth is broad,
> But neither as vast and broad as our party's loving-kindness.
> Father is dear and mother is close,
> But neither as dear and close as Chairman Mao.

– or glorifying the proletarian dictatorship –

To hunt a wolf you need a stick,
To hunt a tiger you need a gun,
To hunt a hidden enemy,
You need the ruthless mind of the revolutionary masses.

When the boy put a record on the turntable, wound it up and placed the needle on the record, I was stunned by the soft sounds I heard. The only words I understood were the translated title on the cover, but the singer's smooth, soulful crooning sounded heavenly to me. It was Nat King Cole singing *Unforgettable.* Then came his *Quizás Quizás Quizás* and *Autumn Leaves*; their melancholy melodies touched my heart.

There was dance music, symphonies, popular songs and jazz. Besides Nat King Cole, I loved Peter Kiesewetter's tango *Pathetique* and Rimsky-Korsakov's *Scheherazade.* It must have been an old recording of the *Pathetique*, with a piano pounding out the rhythm, but for some reason it always made me sad. Was it the memory of my mother as a piano player? Or was it triggered by that desperate but defiant melody?

But I was very clear why I loved *Scheherazade.* Its repeated solo violin theme brought me to tears, of both sadness and joy. I imagined a fragile young girl refusing to surrender to a cruel fate, and was inspired by her victory. I saw myself in her.

The records had been hidden in a dark corner for too long and some were damaged. We would jump as the needle crossed scratches on their mouldy surfaces. Whenever this happened, the boy would remind me again that this was decadent music. "But my father said we need evidence when we criticise capitalism. That's why we still keep them." He was taking a huge risk so he had to protect himself.

Everyone learnt how to rationalise problems in the name of revolution, because throughout that mad decade colleagues, neighbours and family members were encouraged to report on one another. People were trained like sniffer dogs, constantly on the lookout for problems, like the postman who reported my father for distorting Chairman Mao's slogan.

I myself was reported once. In 1971 Chairman Mao called on the nation to undertake field camping and forced marches. Our school did ten days' training on the outskirts of Beijing, and each day we had to walk a minimum of twenty-five kilometres with a full backpack. One day we got lost and ended up walking forty kilometres, so that many of us collapsed and tears flowed freely. I was asked to write a stirring chant for the next day's march to keep everyone's spirits up. I scribbled something like "Forty k's have we done, twenty more should just be fun." Everyone marched along shouting my ballad and no one dropped out. I was proud, but in the evening I was summoned to the school camp headquarters where our deputy principal gave me a formal warning. I had been reported for influencing students to underestimate the enemy by inappropriately comparing our revolutionary training to "fun".

Fortunately there were no such incidents in our courtyard. Though the residents came from different backgrounds, we were closely bound. Even during the Cultural Revolution when people kept themselves at a distance, these bonds were not entirely broken. One explanation was that the thirty-three households had cohabited for more than twenty years and their children had grown up like siblings. But to me, the most important reason was that we had Aunt Li as our yard leader. It was her kind heart and her decency that sustained the healthy bonds in our community. This neighbourhood solidarity may explain why I was able to carry on my storytelling relatively easily; and why it was possible for the boy and me to listen to that "decadent music".

I must point out that storytelling was not rare during those years. Since no books were available, a great deal of oral "literature" circulated openly: political adventures like *An Embroidered Slipper* and *The Plum Flower Party* about the struggles between the Communists and the Kuomintang; love stories like *The Second Handshake* about the unresolved love affair between two scientists; spy stories like *No. 45 Central Street* and even erotic stories such as *The Memoir of Miss*

Manna. Because their politics were sound, these stories were known in most households. But they were unsophisticated, fragmentary and repetitive, and they often made no sense. My stories were based on the classics I had read so they were different and they began to attract adult listeners.

A neighbour from the rear yard, a diplomat who was teaching Chinese language and literature in the French Embassy, walked in one day and asked to join the audience. I was not sure of his motives and worried that, as an adult, he might see something poisonous in Dantès' revenge and report me, so I categorically denied that I had ever told anyone any stories. "The other kids coming to my place? Well, we do homework and … and we criticise capitalist society together," I blustered.

He went to fetch Aunt Li and explained to us both that a French official had asked if he knew any French literature. "Of course I haven't read anything and I don't know where to find it. But I can't say that or our nation will lose face. So I've come to listen to some stories. What do you say? Aunt Li?"

Aunt Li was won over and asked me to do my bit to preserve face for the nation. So the diplomat became a keen listener whose first-hand knowledge of foreigners helped me grasp things beyond my experience. Soon he was known as my storytelling assistant.

People in the diplomatic corps enjoyed quite a few cultural privileges. There was not much entertainment for the Chinese people but there were plenty of special events for foreign guests. This was commonly known and accepted because foreigners were viewed differently. They were bourgeois, after all. The small number of Chinese who enjoyed the same privileges, like my neighbour, had earned them because of their "good origins". The Cultural Revolution had made us accept that, instead of the traditional class divisions based essentially on wealth and education, class divisions in our new China were to be dictated by the proletariat, the workers, peasants and soldiers. People didn't challenge the difference in treatment and conditions, no matter how ridiculous they were. When my neighbour gave me a concert ticket as a thank-you gesture, I just felt lucky.

On 1 May 1973, I was at the Beijing Concert Hall listening to Beethoven's 5th and 7th symphonies. With the four-note opening motif – "dit-dit-dit-dah" – of the 5th, the Fate Symphony, I really felt that "fate was knocking at the door" and my life had come to a pivotal moment. I was completely lost in the music.

At interval I watched people chatting in the foyer, holding glasses of wine or champagne. They were mostly foreigners who had dressed up and were made up beyond my wildest imaginings. I looked out of place in my best shirt with my hair in two neat braids. I could see people wondering what such a poorly dressed girl was doing there. They wouldn't have guessed it was because she could tell stories!

My mother had told me that it was impolite to stare but I could not stop looking at those women with long permed hair. At that time, we could have our hair either shoulder-length or in two braids. Anything fancier was inappropriate and permed hair was strictly forbidden. One of our neighbours had naturally curly hair and one day she returned home with half her head shaved. The Red Guards had punished her for having a perm! Now, one of Chairman Mao's fifteen-year-old girls found herself in a concert hall surrounded by women sporting all kinds of permed and bizarre hair styles!

My thoughts turned to the early days of the Cultural Revolution, not long after my father was sent away. We were spring cleaning with the aim of getting rid of anything that could cause trouble. As a child, I didn't know our real purpose nor could I do much to help, so for me it was like a treasure hunt. I found a colourful silk robe, a delicate cloisonné vase, a small leather briefcase, and a photo of a woman with long permed hair, in a satin dress and standing in her high heels in front of a splendid shop front. It was my mother! Never had I seen her or anyone else looking like that. In the evening, I asked her about the photo. My mother firmly denied that she had ever had such a photo taken. She said I must have been dreaming. I was even challenged to produce the photo, which, of course, could no longer be found.

It was during this interval at the concert that for the first time since her death I recalled my mother's last words: "At least I have lived a life." That life would have included this kind of evening and much more. There existed a very different world from mine.

I began to pin together the elements that had made me see my mother as different from other mothers. She was the most elegantly dressed woman in our residential compound. In the 1960s, people made their own clothes and neighbours came to ask her opinion about colours, materials and styles. Even in an ordinary Mao-style shirt and trousers she stood out with her tall, straight, slim figure. Aunt Li once joked, "Your mother would still look bourgeois wearing a piece of gunnysack." She was also the most knowledgeable person in our compound. People would come to our house seeking answers: What is the meaning of this classical poem? How many passengers can a Boeing 747 seat? Who is Yasser Arafat? Why is Nixon visiting Beijing? And her frequent meaningful talks often lost me!

After the concert, I walked home with a dream: one day, my life would be full of evenings like this. I would be like Pip in Dickens' *Great Expectations*, "graceful and educated", and enjoy the good life my mother had once enjoyed.

Not long after that night, another adult knocked on my door. He was a book illustrator whose son was one of the teenagers listening to my new story, *Great Expectations*. After vainly trying to get the story out of the boy, he had decided to come along himself. To win my trust, he brought a book he had illustrated before the Cultural Revolution, and which was now banned, called *Legends of the Chinese Landscape*. It showcased mountains and great rivers made famous through legends. There were photographs of the natural features accompanied by retellings of ancient legends and his illustrations. "I should have burned them but I didn't. You can report me if I breathe a word about your stories. My son told me they reveal the darkness of capitalist society."

I had heard a lot about the China beyond Beijing from my brother's fellow purchasing agents but this was the first time I had seen images of it. It was breathtaking. The well-known Five Sacred Mountains, the grand Yangtze and Yellow River, picturesque Guilin … they were all too amazing. I remembered my mother's plane trip to Chongqing when she had cheated death. She had had a "fuller life" and had "travelled everywhere"!

I asked this neighbour if he had been to these places and seen them with his own eyes.

"Of course! How else could I get my inspiration?"

My question got him going: "Tell me, when *you* look at these pictures, can you smell anything? Hear anything? Or feel anything?" He gazed into the distance. Then he looked at me again, "Unfortunately you can't. When I was there, in the mountains, by the rivers, the smells, the sounds and the air … Oh, my heart opened up. I just wanted to cry. I was in a different world, in a fairyland, a real one! But I shouldn't say these things to you, they're bourgeois tendencies."

He stopped, but I had already been infected by those tendencies. One day, I told him, even as he shook his head dismissively, I would see those places for myself.

I was finally clear what I needed to save money for. Travel. I longed for new experiences and a different world!

The spring of 1973 not only lifted me out of the cold winter, it also opened my eyes to a world beyond my own. It was the beginning of my quest to live my life as my mother had lived hers.

7
Lonely Traveller

My savings account grew much faster after May. Although I had become a good cook, my meals were mostly cold leftovers. This was a deliberate choice. I cooked only two or three times a week, making enough lazy dragons to last for a couple of days. I drank mainly tap water. In doing so, I saved money on coal briquettes as well as on rice, cooking oil, vegetables and so on. It was much easier to keep to this simple life in the warmer weather and by the end of July I had saved 35 yuan. On 1 August 1973, I boarded the No. 179 train at Beijing station for my first travel adventure.

I had been preoccupied with planning the trip throughout May, June and July. First I had to decide on my destination. Through my book illustrator neighbour I had learnt a lot about China's great mountains, rivers and lakes: the most elegant, Mount Emei; the most sacred, Mount Tai; the most precipitous, Mount Hua; the most powerful river, the Yellow River; the largest lake, Lake Dongting, and so on. I wanted to visit them all but my time and means were limited.

Visiting brothers was a good pretext for travelling. My brother Shu lived in Xi'an, which was near Mount Hua; Yang lived in Sichuan, where Mount Emei was. Xi'an was closer, and cheaper to get to, so I chose Xi'an as my first destination.

At that time, travelling without a work or family-related purpose was almost unheard of. Tourism was a foreign idea and a young girl travelling alone was definitely not normal. But none of this put me off because now I wanted to be different. I didn't tell anyone in my family about my travel plans, not even Shu, whom I was about to visit. I knew my family would worry about my safety, and that from their years of living in poverty they would feel I was frittering money away. I was sure they would try to stop me. Respecting the advice of elders was one of the strict rules I had been raised with, so to avoid being forced to abandon my plans I had kept them secret. I only told Aunt Li at the last minute, after I had locked my house, so that no one would report me as a missing person.

I had done a thorough risk assessment, remembering my mother's oft-repeated advice that danger could be avoided by knowing the risks and preparing well. She had always encouraged me to take risks so my life wouldn't "be dull".

When I was in Grade 1, there was a rowing excursion on the lake at Beihai Park. The parents of many of my classmates decided the activity was too dangerous and kept their children home. My mother, on the other hand, urged me to go. She found the money to buy me a life jacket and ordered my brothers Dong and Jing to give me rowing lessons in the week before the excursion. Only three first graders attended the excursion, and each received a bravery award. I felt special when I shook hands with my principal and was even more thrilled when my mother proudly showed my certificate off to the neighbours. She rarely praised me openly.

Xi'an was a big city and a railroad hub. I had learnt from my brother that there was a No. 14 bus that went straight from Xi'an railway station to his factory. The chances of getting lost were minimal and since my brother lived in one of the factory's apartments, I was sure I would be able to find him easily.

I put on my best shirt and took along a change of clothes, a toothbrush, a piece of soap, and a small towel. The journey would take twenty hours, so I packed a few twisters, four boiled eggs, and a bag of cucumbers and tomatoes to avoid any unnecessary spending on the train. The return train fare for a student from Beijing to Xi'an was 32 yuan. With the 3 yuan remaining from my savings I bought half a dozen sesame cakes, my second-oldest brother's favourite Beijing snack, as a present. My August allowance was delivered on the morning of my departure. I took 15 yuan with me and gave the other half to Aunt Li to cover the rent and to ensure I would have some money left after my return at the end of the month. I was proud that I had thought of everything and was so well prepared.

I arrived at Beijing railway station in the afternoon, extremely excited. I had been there with my mother many times between 1965 and 1969, seeing off my father, Fourth Grandma and my brothers, one after another. Every time the train had started moving and my mother surged towards the carriage calling out her last exhortations, all I could think of was wishing I could be on that train. Once, as the last carriage left the platform, I had voiced this wish and my mother had exploded: "Don't you dare! I've sent everyone else away – don't *you* do that to me too." I knew, though, that she would have been happy for me to go this time because I was going of my own free will.

I had a window seat in a hard-seat carriage. As the train moved off, I opened the window and stuck my head out. I was fascinated by what I saw: the platform receding and vanishing, Beijing station shrinking and fading away. And then rows of trees jumping swiftly into view and falling out of sight while peasants in the distant fields remained almost still.

Two inspectors arrived in the carriage and began checking tickets. I instantly became anxious. By the time they reached me, I was so nervous that my hands shook as I fished out my ticket. They gave me a hard time.

"Who are you travelling with?"

"No one."

"Where are you going?"

"I'm visiting my brother in Xi'an."

"Visiting your brother? Why not your parents?"

I stared at them wordlessly because I wasn't sure how to answer. If I said that my father was in a labour camp, how would they react? Would they send me home?

"Where did you get the money for the ticket? You're sure this is your ticket?"

The ticket was just a two-inch cardboard strip with no passenger's name on it. In the face of my continued silence they began to speak more loudly and their manner became more stern.

Then I heard one of them say, "Refusing to answer questions? Okay, come with us to the office."

Tears filled my eyes and I cried out: "My mother's dead and I want to see my brother. I saved the money myself."

A big man who sat opposite me spoke up, "We can vouch for that. Her mother did die and her brother asked her to spend a holiday in Xi'an. Look at you, bullying a child who has just lost her mother!"

Two or three other passengers echoed his words.

The inspectors looked at each other then said to me, "In future, just answer the questions and then there won't be any problems. There're so many bad elements around nowadays, we can't be too careful. All right, stop crying. If you need anything, let us know."

After they left, I looked at the people sitting around me. There were four middle-aged men in my compartment and most of the passengers in the carriage looked just like colleagues of my oldest brother. Although it was school holidays, there were hardly any students on board. I thanked the big man who had spoken up for me and asked him, "You know my brother?"

He laughed, "Of course not." Then he became serious. "That wasn't a lie about your mother, was it?"

"No, it wasn't. She died last October –"

He put his hand up to stop me saying anything more and asked how old I was. Afterwards, he advised me, "In future, if anyone asks, just say you've lost your mother, and your father and brothers are following Chairman Mao's instructions to work in the developing regions. They're too busy to get away from work so you have to visit them. Understand?"

I understood him perfectly. The Cultural Revolution had not only nurtured plenty of sniffer dogs, it had also trained people in how to protect themselves by manipulating the revolutionary language. I was grateful because he had given me an amulet for my future travels.

By then it was dinner time, and the same railway staff were back, this time pushing trolleys with boxed meals – rice topped with stir-fried dishes. The meals were 30 fen each and smelt very appealing, but I was not going to waste a single fen. I needed money to climb Mount Hua. I took out two twisters, one egg and one cucumber for my dinner.

While the others enjoyed their boxed meals, I turned to face the window and ate quietly. Just before I finished the first twister, the big man called out to me. "Hey you, you selfish girl. You're hiding good food from us. That's not nice, not nice at all." He shook his head theatrically. "My boxed meal for one of your twisters?"

I looked at him as if he was mad but he simply handed over an unopened boxed meal and took my second twister. "I'm a northerner and I love buns, pancakes and twisters. I hope you don't mind."

Of course I didn't mind – a boxed meal cost five times more than a twister! Before I could say a word, he had bitten into the twister and said, "Too late, now you have to eat my boxed meal."

It was so delicious that I felt I was eating at a restaurant. I had met a good person who had taken pity on me. To show my gratitude, I collected the empty boxes after everyone had finished, cleared away the rubbish, and replenished with hot water the two bottles in our compartment for making tea. The big man kept praising me to the others, "See, what a sensible child this is. If only her mother could see her … alas, Heaven is not fair!"

His kind words brought tears to my eyes, and made me wish my mother were there to see me on this, my first adventure. I headed out of the carriage to the toilet to hide my emotions.

The first lengthy stop was Baoding. Most of the travellers got off to wander along the platform during the fifteen-minute stop. Baoding was my mother's hometown. I wanted to see it even if only from the platform, but I did not dare get off the train, fearful it would suddenly pull away without me.

It was an old station. From the train window, I could see a big gate on the far side of the platform engraved with the date of its construction, 1899. Many passengers had passed through it, my mother among them. I visualised her as a young student, in a white blouse and black skirt, hurrying through the gate and boarding a train towards her future; and then as a successful woman, with long permed hair, elegantly walking back through the gate on her return home. I wanted to follow in her footsteps, except for marrying someone like my father.

The thought of this marriage and her troubles with Old Mushroom brought my daydreaming to an end and I turned my attention to the dimly lit platform. It was very wide. A few station workers were pushing trolleys laden with food, cigarettes and newspapers to sell to the passengers. I got excited when I saw one of the trolleys was piled high with Salt and Pepper Cake – Baoding's specialty. I had tasted it before at Uncle Yuji's house and my mother had told me that it was her favourite childhood snack. "Next time," I promised myself, "I'll buy some."

The stationmaster blew the whistle and the train moved off again. The big man and his colleagues returned with bags of smoked chicken and other Baoding specialties, but no cake.

"I've bought a new edition so you can have this one." The big man handed me a booklet entitled *China Nationwide Train Timetable*. I had seen it before – my father had one.

"It looks old but it's perfectly okay. You do need to stretch your legs whenever there's a chance. If you sit too long without moving, your feet can swell up. With this timetable, you won't miss the train. But don't forget, you must take your valuables with you." He turned to the timetable for the No. 179 train and showed me how to use it. "See here, the next long stop is at Shijiazhuang, where we'll stop for twenty minutes. You should get off with us."

"Thank you." I took the booklet and gave him a big smile. If I got off with them, I'd be safe. I looked forward to it, to seeing the train from outside and to walking in a strange place.

But I did not get off at Shijiazhuang because I fell asleep. I was exhausted. For weeks I had been preoccupied by this trip; I had worried so much that something would go wrong that I had become obsessed with my preparations. I had cleaned the house, washed the bedding, tightened up every grain bag to prevent grubs from sneaking in, and calculated my money again and again. I had originally budgeted 10 yuan for visiting Mount Hua, which was two hundred kilometres from Xi'an according to my neighbour's book, and 5 yuan for my brother – I was going to stay in his house for three weeks.

Then I wondered if that was too selfish. Should it be 9 yuan and 6? Or 8 and 7? It was exhausting trying to work out what was best. On top of all the preparations, I had had to behave as normally as possible with the neighbours so no one would guess I was about to leave. My mother had told me to never tell lies, so I had kept a low profile to avoid questions that might force me to reveal the truth, because if I did that then my family would know. For nearly a month, it felt as if I was living underground. The night before my journey I did not sleep at all.

On the train I woke up suddenly and for a couple of minutes had no idea where I was. Gradually, the rhythmic noises and the occasional faint whistles made me realise I was not dreaming but was actually travelling. I relaxed and relished the moment. Then I heard soft voices and turned to see that the big man was telling a story to his colleagues. I sat up straight, and they suddenly stopped.

"I know you're telling stories and I want to listen too." I was encouraged to make this demand by the special care he had shown to me.

The big man replied, "You've been dreaming. We're not telling stories; we're criticising capitalist societies!"

"That's what I meant," I said. "And after you finish yours, I'll tell you one."

The big man was telling a story I had never heard before: "You Are

My Sun". It was about two orphaned brothers, one a talented artist, the other a singer. They were too poor to both receive an education so the older brother lied, saying that he was studying at a faraway college with a scholarship generous enough to support them both, thereby sacrificing his future, his youth and his health to support his younger brother, the singer. When they finally met ten years later, one a celebrity, the other a poor cripple, the singer sang, "You Are My Sun".

The big man concluded, "See how people suffer under capitalism. If they had lived in our new China, they would both have been successful."

This was my chance to tell O. Henry's "The Gift of the Magi".

"I absolutely agree," I said. "Let me tell you a story that happened in imperial America. It reveals the sordid state of capitalism."

My words, just like the big man's were automatic, but I also believed what I was saying – the evil of capitalism was a given for us. It was a fact like the rising of the sun.

My telling of "The Gift of the Magi", the story of a young couple's struggle to find money to buy gifts for each other, was a success. In the story Della sells her beautiful long hair to buy her husband, Jim, a fob chain for his pocket watch, his only valuable possession, but Jim has sold his watch to buy combs for his wife to put in her hair. My listeners felt so sorry for the young couple when I finished and spent a long time debating alternative endings to their story.

"Your story is good," one of them said, "but it's too cruel."

"Well, that's capitalist society for you," I said triumphantly, grinning broadly.

When the big man and his colleagues got off at Zhengzhou, he left me half a smoked chicken, and drew me a detailed map of Xi'an railway station, telling me that I must always approach three people for directions to avoid getting the wrong information. "I'd be cross if my daughter travelled on her own," he kept saying.

I asked for his contact details so I could let him know I was okay. He refused. "Don't be upset," he said to me. "It's not personal. Nowadays, the fewer people you know, the better. You should be more aware of this too." He turned to me as he got off the train. "I hope you haven't forgotten how those inspectors interrogated you. Do be careful."

Standing on the platform, I watched them disappear and suddenly felt very alone. With its many shops and goods for sale, Zhengzhou station appeared far more dazzling than Baoding but I had no interest in exploring it. Surrounded by strangers, I felt vulnerable with no one to protect me anymore. I returned to my seat. Silently repeating the big man's parting advice, I didn't utter a word to anyone for the rest of the journey.

It was mid-morning when I arrived in Xi'an. Following the crowd and copying the other travellers, I passed through the exit gate and found myself standing in a big square. Turning around, I saw on top of the station façade the two big red characters: 西安 Xi'an. My heart leapt – I'd made it! I took a few deep breaths to calm down and took out the big man's map. I couldn't claim success until I walked into my brother's home. As my mother had often said, "For a journey of a hundred miles, one should count ninety as half-way."

"Why?" I had asked.

"The last bit is often the hardest," she had explained.

I found the No. 14 bus easily and felt relieved to learn that it terminated at the Lucky Village stop, where my brother lived and worked. I didn't need to worry about getting off too early or too late.

Today in Xi'an, Lucky Village is a prime inner-city location, but in the early 1970s it was on the outskirts. I was disappointed to see that for more than half the journey the bus ran alongside farmland. Xi'an Chemical Factory was in the middle of a village.

I was sent to two or three different workshops before someone finally told me that my brother was on nightshift that week and would be at home sleeping. I followed a worker to the third floor of a concrete building and stood at his door. I suddenly wondered – would he be happy to see me? Or would he be angry at my unannounced visit? Seeing me hesitate, the worker knocked, "Bi Xishu, open the door, you have a guest."

Shu opened the door, still half asleep. He froze when he saw me and then tears poured down his face.

He hadn't seen any members of the family since my mother's death. Deeply in debt for the money he had borrowed to get everyone home when my mother died, he hadn't been able to think about anything else. My arrival opened the floodgate of his pent-up emotions. And mine too. Instead of feeling triumphant at having got there on my own, I burst into tears as well. Goodness knows what the worker who had brought me to Shu's door thought!

I stayed with Shu more than three weeks. Every day when he and his wife went to work, I toured the neighbourhood with my nephew – the one I had helped my mother look after for two years. It was school holidays so with me there my brother didn't have to pay for holiday care for his son. I didn't mind because I had a special bond with this nephew whom I had heard utter his first word and seen take his first steps. However, I didn't find this provincial city particularly interesting. The first weekend, my brother took me out to Xingqing Park, Xi'an's biggest, a large garden with an artificial lake; the second weekend he took me to Wild Goose Pagoda, the tomb of Xuanzang, the monk who brought the Buddhist classics to China in the seventh century; and on my last weekend he took me to the Bell Tower, a 600-year-old structure in the city centre with the biggest bell in China.

Having grown up next to the imperial garden of Beihai Park, Xingqing Park did not have much appeal for me and I was too young to be interested in historic sites. In my time with my brother I became a family helper, carrying coal briquettes to their fourth-floor apartment, or buying grain from the co-op. I ate well and enjoyed their company, but I was bored and, in particular, I didn't get to visit Mount Hua.

Shu did not believe in spending money for the sake of seeing beautiful things. When I mentioned Mount Hua on the first day, he replied firmly, "No. I have neither the money nor the time to go with you." When I said I had the money and could go by myself, he sat me down and explained, "A trip to Mount Hua, including tickets and an overnight stay in a mountain hut, will cost 7 yuan, at least. For that much money, a worker in my factory can buy a monthly mess card and you can buy a new shirt and a pair of new trousers. Does that really make sense to you?"

He made it clear that I was not being sensible, but I was not convinced. I had saved the money, cent by cent, and a trip to Mount Hua made a great deal of sense to me. Secretly, I pitied him and thought that he had become a terrible bore.

Before 1966, when he had been working in Beijing Chemical Factory, Shu had not been a bore. He was my mother's favourite son, not only because he was loving and responsible, but also because he had a romantic view of life. His work involved dangerous chemicals, so he was paid very well. He had his hair cut in a salon, not a barber shop, shopped for the newest fashions in Beijing Department Store, not the local co-op, and spent his weekends with friends at picnics or banquets. He *had* spent money on beautiful but "senseless" things: a stylish radio, a plaster bust of a young girl, an embroidered tablecloth and decorative animal figurines. He had even taken me to the salon to have my hair bobbed. I had looked up to him and always enjoyed going out with him because he was lots of fun.

His unusual lifestyle had attracted the attention of some of the neighbours. Aunt Li had voiced to my mother their concerns about Shu's bourgeois tendencies, and my mother had assured the yard leader that she would watch Shu carefully. But behind closed doors, my mother had expressed pleasure at Shu's "fuller life": "If he doesn't enjoy life now," she said, "when will he?" Now, years of hardship had obliterated Shu's romantic sensibilities and rectified his bourgeois tendencies.

He now lived a very bland life, three meals a day, queuing for discounted vegetables after work, checking his budget every evening. He rarely smiled and often exploded over trivial issues. I couldn't wait to return to Beijing.

On the night before my departure, he stayed up late making red bean sweet buns for me to take on the road. He was in tears. "I'm sorry about Mount Hua. Next time, I promise –" he began, but he stopped there. He didn't know if he could deliver on any promises. My resentment faded when I saw his tears. However, my view of his life didn't change. Although I knew his lifestyle was not entirely his choice – he had been forced to leave Beijing because of our blemished family and to settle for a minimum wage – I couldn't help feeling critical of him.

My months of hard saving, my meticulous planning and my dream of seeing a different world turned out to be in vain. On the way home, I was so disappointed that I had no desire to talk to anyone on the train. Only one thought occupied my mind: *I'll do anything to avoid living like Shu.*

8

The World Opens Up to Me

Neighbours, young and old, asked about my trip when I returned to Beijing – Aunt Li had spread the news. No one made any critical remarks like Shu had. Instead of "spending money senselessly", I heard "brave", "capable", "organised" and "smart." People admired me for being able to do something out of the ordinary. My spirits revived. When neighbouring kids asked me to tell them about my trip, I described the interior of the train, my fellow travellers, the taste of the boxed meal, the different stations and the dull city of Xi'an.

Travel made me the compound celebrity. My peers suddenly envied me my orphan status for the freedom it seemed to give me. For years I had wished I were like the other children – had their kind of family and wore their kinds of clothes – but now I felt superior in my difference.

Only the illustrator made a dispiriting comment: "You went that far without climbing Mount Hua? What a waste!"

I didn't offer any defence but secretly vowed, *Next year, I'll be on top of Mount Emei!*

The following year, 1974, my life was smooth and incident free. At school, I kept top place in the academic rankings and I read many more banned classics. At home, the house was clean, the stove was rarely dead, and my cooking was "better than the mother's", according to Aunt Li. My overwhelming memories of that year, though, are all about money.

I spent every month from September 1973 to July 1974 saving

money. On the first day of every month, I put 6 yuan into the bank immediately after Mr Li delivered my allowance. When my savings reached 50 yuan, the local bank manager came out from behind the counter to shake my hand. He told me that I was the youngest account holder in the neighbourhood. I was proud but I didn't drop my guard when he asked me the purpose of my saving.

"I lost my mother, and my father and brothers are following Chairman Mao's instructions to work in the developing regions. They're too busy to get away from work so I have to save money to visit them." I hadn't forgotten the big man's advice.

The bank manager praised my "high class consciousness". I wished I could tell him my true purpose, but if my own brother scorned my dreams of travel, a bank manager, a money man, would likely think the same way. I didn't want to hear any disparaging comments or create potential obstacles.

I had a fight with Dong over money. He returned home more often in 1974 and on 1 May, Labour Day, he brought a girl home but found he had forgotten his wallet. He was embarrassed because he had promised to take her out to a restaurant. Then he found the 6 yuan I had put in the desk drawer until I could put it in the bank after the holiday. When I found the money gone the next morning, I yelled at him and refused to accept his explanation. Dong was hurt and made the two-hour bus trip back to his place to get his wallet and replace the money. I cried when he handed it over, regretting my mean behaviour. In taking control of my life, I had already become obsessive and rigid.

When the summer holidays of 1974 arrived, I took off to Sichuan – and Mount Emei – where my oldest brother lived. Sichuan was on the other side of the Qinling Mountains, the natural border between north and south China, and its landscapes and culture were exotic. Moreover, Sichuan was famous for its delicious and affordable food. I was thrilled to be going there. Even if my brother forbade me to visit Emei on my own, I would see the south and that was something extraordinary for me.

From a very young age, I had heard the south of China described as a paradise. Born into a musical family, I grew up listening to songs. In the early 1960s, these were mostly about developing the far west and northeast, always with the promise that this remote corner or that barren desert would soon be as beautiful as the fabled south. These songs taught me that the south was neither cold nor hot, that its trees were evergreen. Its sky was bluer, its flowers redder, and its women prettier. My favourite song was *Ascending Lofty Mount Xingan*:

> Ascending lofty Mount Xingan,
> Through the vast meadowland where I herd cattle and sheep,
> I imagine the poetic landscape of the south
> And smell the southern blossoms.

My brother Yang lived in Hanwang, a small town with a population of 20,000 nestled against Mount Dragon and in a meander of the Mian River. No one would have gone there had the Chinese government not made it the site of the Oriental Turbine Factory. This brought in thousands of workers from all over the country. There was no direct train to Hanwang, so I had to change at Deyang, a couple of stops before Chengdu, the capital of Sichuan province.

After a gruelling 36-hour journey I got off the train at Deyang and was surprised to see my brother waiting on the platform. He was supposed to pick me up at Hanwang. "Oh, changing trains in Deyang can be complicated. The regional trains are not punctual and you may not be able to understand the Sichuan accent," he said, taking my bag. "You're getting taller. I'm afraid your sister-in-law won't recognise you."

I had not seen him since my mother's death, and this was the first mention of my sister-in-law, whom I had not seen for nearly five years. I had unpleasant memories of my sister-in-law yelling at my mother about her proletarian rights; railing against my mother's bourgeois manners; not to mention, of my brother reporting my mother and me. Silently, I reaffirmed a resolution I had made before coming: if they were mean to me, I would leave and move into a hotel for a few days. I had saved double the amount I had taken with me to Xi'an. I could afford it if I had to.

Yang had combined business with this personal mission to collect me, so during the hour-long wait for the train to Hanwang I wandered around the station while he was out and about busily dealing with work. It was small and clean, with a row of flowering trees, intermixed with sweet-scented oleander and hibiscus, in the middle of the platform. Even in deep summer, their red petals and green leaves appeared fresh and bright in the moist air.

Everything looked different: the shops, both inside and outside the station, were like rooms without front walls. I wondered how they could be locked up after business hours. The people, their clothes, their headgear and their backpack baskets were foreign to me. They spoke loudly with heavy accents and dramatic cadences that sounded like they were arguing. Xi'an had been nothing like this. I felt very privileged to be able to travel there.

When we boarded the single carriage local train, I leant against the window to get a good view. The train track ran beside a vast paddy field covered with water, where green rice shoots were being planted. It was like a huge mirror reflecting the sky, the clouds and the moving train. Here and there I saw farmers bending over planting rice shoots. There was no winter in Sichuan, my brother told me, so they had three rice crops a year. On the other side of the railway track was a small creek in which boys were riding on the backs of buffaloes. This creek, Yang said, flowed through the grassland behind his house.

It was a twenty-minute walk along the town's main street, Horse Tail Lane, from the railway station to my brother's house. The street was a kilometre long, narrow, twisting and crowded. It was market day and hundreds of local villagers were lined up on both sides of the street. They had marked off their "shop fronts" with their carrying poles to sell whatever they had in their two bamboo baskets. They shouted and waved things at the passing crowd.

I was astonished to see what they were selling – not only an abundance of fresh and exotic vegetables, but also meat, eggs, tofu and cooking oil, items that were strictly rationed in Beijing.

My brother pulled a small bag of rice from his briefcase and exchanged it for a slice of pork shoulder from a meat seller. "Your sister-in-law will cook this for you tonight," he explained, as my jaw dropped.

I said nothing because every Beijinger knew bartering rationed goods was as illegal as selling them on the black market. My brother could be jailed if he was found out! I was scared for him and looked around to see if anyone had noticed.

Yang laughed, "Don't worry. This is not Beijing. We all do this. Haven't you heard the saying 'Heaven is high and the emperor is far'?"

I was amazed. I really had come to a different world!

Behind the row of carrying-pole "shops" were the proper shops, in solid buildings: the bank, the post office, the government-owned co-op department store and a few small restaurants. I did not recognise most of the foods in the restaurant windows but I could smell them and they smelled very appetising indeed.

Yang took me into one of the restaurants and ordered me a big bowl of short soup – "dragon's claws" they called it. It was basically dumplings in soup. Because "dragons must eat seafood", my brother explained, "the filling is shrimp meat mixed with vegetables". The dumpling wrapper was paper thin, the filling generous, and the soup was full of fried tofu and tiny fresh mushrooms. I had never tasted anything so delicious and I knew I had truly arrived in paradise.

Yang's home was in a semicircle of twenty single-storey terraces that faced vast rice fields, fishponds and stone bridges; it was a very beautiful setting. The township of Hanwang was at the bottom of the Sichuan basin, so there was water everywhere. Behind my brother's house was the creek I had seen from the train, but here it ran with quite a force. My brother warned me to be careful. "If you fall in, you'll be carried away to Mount Emei and eventually into the grand Yangtze."

"Really?" I was excited. "This river connects to Emei and to the Yangtze!" I exclaimed, and smiled at Yang.

On the train, I had told him of my desire to climb Mount Emei and he had straightaway said, "No … Too far. It's a two-hour bus trip to the base of the mountain. It's the biggest mountain in China and it takes at least three days to climb to the top. I can't let you go by yourself, and I won't go with you, spending money to buy suffering."

Although he said this in a light-hearted manner, I had been very upset and didn't speak again until we were walking down the main street. By then I was so pleased with what I had seen that I told myself it would not be so terrible if I missed Emei this time.

There were more pleasant surprises awaiting me in Yang's house. My sister-in-law seemed transformed. When she lived with us in Beijing, she was seen as a lazy and unruly daughter-in-law: she didn't lift a finger to do housework, not even to make her own bed, and she'd fought with my fifth-oldest brother, Jing, and me over food.

Now I walked into a spotless house and a warm welcome. As well as the fine room she had prepared for me, she had bought fabric to make me a short-sleeved shirt, a sleeveless dress, and a light jacket.

"You can sew?" I asked in disbelief. When my mother had been teaching me sewing, this woman had slammed her for reinforcing feudal ideas in the younger generation.

"Yes. I made your brother's shirts and trousers," she answered proudly, not picking up the innuendo behind my question.

For the next ten days, every day after work my sister-in-law would cook, wash, clean, and then sit late into the night sewing my new clothes. On 12 August, the eve of my birthday, she cooked a huge dinner of grilled fish, stir-fried shrimps and braised chicken, and presented me with the three neatly folded garments.

"But my birthday is tomorrow!" I said in embarrassment.

"Tomorrow?" she said, winking at my brother, "Tomorrow there'll be no food here for you."

"Why?" I turned to my brother, but his wife blurted out the answer for him. "Tomorrow you'll have dinner on Mount Emei!"

"What?" I turned to my brother again. "Is that true?"

"Well, your sister-in-law said she'd divorce me if I didn't take you to Mount Emei."

I looked at my sister-in-law and my brother, too stunned to come up with any response.

The two of them burst out laughing.

During dinner, I asked her bluntly why she was being so kind. She was not offended but replied tearfully, "There's an old saying, the oldest sister-in-law is a substitute for a lost mother. I lost my mother when I was nine and I suffered because I didn't have an older sister-in-law. Now I must in turn be good to you to ease your suffering."

She had struggled tirelessly against old ideas when she was a Red Guard, but the old ideas still persisted in her. Perhaps Mao's instructions could not triumph over old ideas that were grounded in fundamental human decency!

One of the lasting effects of Mao's revolution was the damage it did to the bonds between children and parents, husbands and wives, teachers and students, neighbours, colleagues and siblings. This led to many estrangements during the Cultural Revolution that endure to this day.

My sister-in-law had been one of these victims. After my mother's death, she had tried to reconcile with our family but died before she was fully forgiven. I was the only one who kept contact with her, because of her kindness during that visit. Even so, I could not forget the way she had burst into our world in her belted Red Guard uniform and the class warfare she had waged against our mother. The scars were too fresh.

Mount Emei is 3,400 metres above sea level. Back then – before there were cable cars – it took most people three days to climb to the peak, the Golden Crest. Although the ancient mountain trek was paved with stone slabs and was not at all steep or rough, my calves were terribly sore after six hours of climbing to Wannian Temple, the first major stop.

Initially, my brother was astonished by the grand scale of the mountain and thanked me for taking him there. By the time we got to the temple gate, however, he was not quite so enthusiastic. "This really is spending money to buy suffering," he said, slumped against the gate. But, for me, the sore calves were worth it, and I walked all around the temple in the last bit of daylight, in high spirits.

About forty people had climbed to Wannian Temple that day. I was surprised to see most of them either bowing or praying as the day turned to dusk, defying the government's anti-religion policy by worshipping at this holy Buddhist site. Like the bartering of rationed food in the main street of Hanwang, such scenes wouldn't be countenanced in Beijing.

My brother called me over to him. It was dinner time and we would have dinner with the monks. Everyone had a bowl of rice topped with pickled vegetables, which cost 10 fen. We sat in the temple courtyard, the evening mist curling up from below. Imagining myself a superior being, I ate with great relish. My brother stopped complaining and enjoyed the meal too.

After dinner, we were herded into the middle hall, where we were to sleep on the stone floor. The monks gave everyone a straw mattress and a blanket but there were no lights, so when the monks left with their oil lamps it was pitch black. I could not see a thing.

Someone whispered, "This must be what hell looks like."

Another responded, "How do you know if you can't see anything?"

My brother was so exhausted that he fell asleep immediately, but I stared into the dark the whole night. My exhilaration turned into dismay. I had never experienced such darkness and it played tricks on my mind. I felt I was alone in an unknown world. Even the snoring and people talking in their sleep right next to me felt remote. The darkness seemed to have volume and weight, and it pressed down on me. I held my body against the floor to avoid being crushed by it. I kept imagining Dumas's Dantès in the dungeon of the Château d'If, where it must have been dark like this. When the first faint light filtered into the temple, I remembered Dantès' escape. Only then did I eventually fall asleep.

I woke to find the temple and the whole mountain it was on engulfed in fog so heavy that the monks had to run a rope from the middle hall to the toilet to the front gate of the temple to help us move about. I fumbled to the front gate, stood there and inhaled deeply, trying to experience what my neighbour, the illustrator, had experienced – "the smells, the sounds and the air … Oh, I just wanted to cry."

The same emotions were now flowing through me. I could see nothing but I felt the air moving around me, I smelled the forest and heard voices seemingly from far away. I might have been too young to realise how insignificant my day-to-day struggles were in the great scheme of things, but the seed of such ideas was planted in me that morning. That was the moment my curiosity about worlds unknown was ignited.

Because of the fog, we did not reach the top of the mountain, but my trip to Sichuan and my experience on Mount Emei had made me feel like a seasoned traveller.

On my way home from Sichuan I began to think about where I might travel to in 1975. I could go east to climb Mount Tai to view its famous sunrise, or I could go to the Hukou Falls to experience the powerful Yellow River, or I could go through the spectacular Three Gorges of the Yangtze River. It was nice to fantasise, but soon after my return to Beijing I realised that all this was unaffordable because of the cost of accommodation. Also, this year I had other needs so I wouldn't be able to save as much.

After my seventeenth birthday, I suddenly grew so much that most of my old clothes would no longer fit me. The long-sleeved shirt that my mother had made was worn out. All of the clothes my sister-in-law had made me were for the hot summer. I had also become more conscious of how I looked. I realised I had to spend some money on new clothes and shoes.

Although interest in the opposite sex was labelled as having a "complicated mind" and puppy love could be treated as a juvenile crime, once they entered the final year of high school most of my classmates had begun to pay attention to their appearance. One way to avoid criticism was to dress up en masse. Ling was the leader of the girls in our class. One day she would issue the order "Tomorrow we will all wear a floral skirt" and on another she would say "Everyone put on a bright scarf with a white shirt." She was frequently annoyed with me because I didn't have most of the items she demanded we wear so she had a heart-to-heart talk with me.

"Listen to this old saying," she said. "'Horses shine in their saddles, people in their clothes.' We're in our last year and can't afford to get around school in shabby clothes. You're a very important figure in our class and you shouldn't do anything to lower our class image. Have a look at what the others are wearing."

I looked around at the colourful skirts and down at my bland old trousers and faded shirt. I suddenly felt very low.

"I can lend you money if you need it. My mother paid me for knitting my brothers' sweaters," Ling kindly offered.

"No, no. Thank you so much but I have money." I would never borrow money again.

So I bought myself a pair of dark grey polyester trousers, a new long-sleeved shirt and two scarves, one for the winter and another for the warmer weather. I also bought a pair of slip-on cotton shoes. Buying a new shirt was my most difficult task. Pink shirts were still the fashion for young girls, but I didn't want pink. My mother had said it did not go well with my dark skin. I searched many co-ops and finally chose a shirt with a fine maroon, navy blue and ginger check. All of this swallowed up nearly 30 yuan of my savings but I did feel wonderful when I put on the new garments, particularly when I heard the book illustrator say, "You have good taste."

My good taste was confirmed by another neighbour who was a professional photographer. He took me and his daughter to his studio to take a photo of us. "Your new look deserves this," he said. He asked us to braid our hair neatly and to run our tongue over our lips to wet them. "No one is allowed to use lipstick nowadays," he said, "but this will create a similar effect in a black and white photo." I stood behind his daughter and we both smiled shyly for the photo. I was pleased with the way I looked and from that moment on became conscious about my appearance.

It wasn't just lack of money that affected my travel plans; time was an issue, too. My last year of senior high school was 1975. Although there was no university to go to, we still had to sit the final exam in November to graduate. Many of my classmates asked me to help them during the summer holiday.

Nevertheless, I was determined to have a short trip. After consulting my book-illustrator neighbour, I chose to go to Henan to see Mount Yuntai, less grand but most mysterious for its fairy-tale landscape. It was only six hundred kilometres from Beijing so the train fare was cheap. Furthermore, it was right next to my father's home village where Fourth Grandma now lived. Although my family had not had any contact with her since she had been sent back to the village in 1966, we knew through other relatives that she had settled into an old abandoned house. I wrote asking if I could stay with her and her one-line reply was: "Yes, yes, yes! I miss you and come soon."

As a child, I had been very close to Fourth Grandma and had often fallen asleep in her bed listening to her fascinating folk tales. Dong, Jing, and I, the three youngest she had looked after, had regarded her as our own grandma. She regarded my parents as her saviours because they had taken her in after the Land Reform. Her love for us and her loyalty to our family were unconditional.

When she was sent home in October 1966, my mother, Dong, Jing and I went to see her off at Beijing railway station. Our mother had explained to us why this was necessary: "Your father's problem is likely to bring the Red Guards to our home. If they uncover Fourth Grandma's past, we will all be in bigger trouble." Still, we all, Mother included, felt guilty about her going because it was fifteen years since Fourth Grandma had left the village and she no longer had any relatives there. She might not survive.

The last time we had been at the railway station was in September to farewell Shu when he left for Xi'an. Much had changed in just a month. Two huge banners now hung from ceiling to floor. One read, "Never forget class struggle!" and the other, "Don't let a single enemy go unpunished!"

The departure gates to the platforms were upstairs and Red Guards had gathered in front of the escalators, staircases and lifts, checking passengers' identification and asking their reasons for leaving Beijing. I was alarmed by the frightened looks on my mother's and brothers' faces. Before anyone could react, some Red Guards ushered us into the queue for the gate to Henan, Fourth Grandma's destination.

Waiting our turn to be interrogated, we saw that most of the others in the queue were older family members leaving Beijing to avoid trouble, just like Fourth Grandma. Some had family to see them off, others were by themselves. One frail old man was being questioned by two Red Guards.

"Why are you leaving Beijing?" a female guard yelled at him.

"I want to live in my hometown, in Zhengzhou," the man muttered.

"Have you gone back often?"

"No. I haven't been back for twenty years." The man clearly couldn't lie.

"Why now?"

"I – my family feels –" his voice dropped and he looked around desperately.

"You want to escape. No way!" The male guard stepped over, handcuffed him and dragged him away.

Terrified, no one in the queue uttered a word. Dong whispered, "Let's go home."

Jing replied, "Too late. Look!"

We were now sandwiched between two rows of Red Guards. I hid behind my mother, who clutched my hand tightly. The blood had drained from her face.

It was Fourth Grandma who said quietly, "No need to worry. Everything is predestined." She was a small woman with a kind, round face that always wore a shy, almost girlish smile. We had never seen her lose her equanimity. When the two Red Guards questioned her, she replied in her soft voice, "I need to go back to my home village to get my bound feet treated. They are terribly painful. There's no one who can do it in Beijing. I have to go back regularly."

The Red Guard let her go. On our way home, we were too amazed to comment. My mother finally said, "Fourth Grandma survived the Land Reform; she'll be fine."

Fourth Grandma paid a villager to pick me up from Yueshan railway station. It was the day before my eighteenth birthday. When I arrived, she was standing outside her door waiting, leaning against the doorframe to relieve the pressure on her tiny bound feet. She looked exactly the same but she seemed to have shrunk. Her smile erased the near decade-long distance between us. I fell into her arms just like before.

She couldn't stop smiling as she ushered me inside. "You're so tall, your hair is so thick, and you look so smart." She touched my cheeks, held my hands and ordered me to turn around so she could have a good look at me. Then she began to cry. "I just feel sorry for your mother," she said. "She'd be so proud …" She dried her eyes and changed the subject as she led me to the kitchen. "Now, come and see what I've cooked for your birthday."

The kitchen was just a corner of a big multipurpose room and comprised a stove, a water pot, a small timber cabinet and a brick bench. On the bench was a pot of stewed meat, a salad of water-lily shoots, and my favourite deep-fried gold and silver butterfly-shaped dim sums. A big watermelon was cooling in the water pot.

"Fourth Grandma, you're spoiling me!" I cried with joy.

"Yes, I am. I'll make you different dishes every day, whatever you fancy. Have you seen my garden?"

She led me outside again.

She shared a U-shaped country cottage with a young couple and their child who had been deported from Zhengzhou, the capital of Henan province, for political reasons. They occupied two-thirds of the building and she had two rooms on one side. A 30-square-metre section of the yard in front of her rooms was fenced off with bamboo lattices. This was her garden. In it were green cucumbers, red tomatoes, golden pumpkins, dark purple eggplants, and many more things I couldn't name. It was very pretty as evening drew in.

"Fourth Grandma, your garden is like a paradise," I exclaimed, as I touched the various vines and vegetables.

Pleased by my reaction, she pointed out a few hens that were scratching around in the garden and led me to a pile of hay. "Put your hand in there and see what you can find. Be careful." I did and found four eggs. "Laid today, very fresh," she said as she took them from me. "I'll make you egg pancakes tonight. You go and get washed and changed, and then we'll eat."

That night, I slept with Fourth Grandma just as I had when I was a little girl. Holding her hand, I enjoyed feeling that I was not alone and was loved. Her bedroom was simple – a double bed, a trunk and a chair – but her bedding was fresh and clean and smelled of sunshine. She told me about her life in the village.

She had been lucky, she said, that she had found these two long-abandoned rooms soon after her return to the village. In the first few years, she worked as a field labourer, like the other villagers, for her food. Now, in her seventies, she was too old for farm labour and her previous status as a concubine made her ineligible for retirement benefits, so she had set up her garden, with the hens, so that she could exchange vegetables and eggs for staple foods and pocket money. She also cooked banquets for village events, sewed wedding garments and grave clothes for other families. "People have got used to me and I'm doing fine. And now that you've come to visit me, I have nothing to complain about."

She had summed up ten years of her life in ten minutes in a matter-of-fact manner. But I was old enough to know how much hostility she would have faced when she returned to the village, how incredibly hard it must have been to make this abandoned ruin liveable, and how tight her current situation was. I swore to her that I would get her back to Beijing as soon as I began to earn money.

Fourth Grandma offered me a paradise within her cosy home and heavenly garden, but I saw misery as soon as I stepped beyond there. I saw the pigsty home of her neighbours, the dispirited young couple, when I delivered a bag of Beijing candies for their child; and I witnessed the mother tying her toddler to a tree while she went off to work the long day through. The child crawled around, staggered about in the dirt, picked up rubbish to stuff into his mouth, bumped up against walls and trees, and cried till he was exhausted. She had left a bucket of water and a plate of cold buns for him at the door. The sight of this recalled what my mother had said when Yang had tried to have us deported: "Do you know what it means to be deported to a remote village?" Now I knew what it meant, and I realised I was not the most unlucky child in the world.

"I help whenever I can but it's not easy," Fourth Grandma said to me as she pressed a piece of meat into the child's hand, "because we've both had political problems and there may be trouble if people see us associating with one another."

Three days later, I left Fourth Grandma and headed to Mount Yuntai. Leaving her was very hard. We both fought back tears while saying reassuring things like, "I'll come to visit you again," "I'll make you more delicacies." She leaned against the door waving and suddenly looked very frail. I worried that I might not see her again.

The same villager who had picked me up delivered me to the foot of Mount Yuntai. On the way he told me, "Your Fourth Grandma is the most generous and gracious person. The whole village loves her. But we have to be careful not to get too close to her. She too must watch her words and deeds. You know how it is, this is the Cultural Revolution."

He also told me that our family had always been in Fourth Grandma's thoughts, imagining how tall the children would be and whether they ate well. When my mother died, she had gone out to a field, burned some incense and cried. Someone reported this to the village revolutionary committee as "suspicious behaviour" and she had been locked up for a day for carrying out feudal rituals.

Tears ran down my face. None of us had given her a thought after she left Beijing. Only when I wanted to see Mount Yuntai had I remembered Fourth Grandma. I felt so guilty.

Mount Yuntai was charming with its twisting paths and waterfalls, but I preferred wild and grand views. The only interesting part of the tour for me was seeing local villagers secretly selling water, fruit, homemade pancakes and woven bamboo handicrafts on the mountain. One man was selling animal figures which he carved out of peach pits on the spot. I was amazed by his skill and sat beside him watching him create his figures. He also told the fortunes of those who bought his wares.

"Aren't you worried?" I asked him after he had just predicted a young man's future and put the 30 fen fee away.

"About what? Spreading superstition?" he said, laughing. "No. My superstitious nonsense stays on the mountain."

"Are your predictions accurate?"

"Hundred per cent," he bragged and explained how he observed people carefully and knew what they were thinking from the way they asked their questions, their reactions to his responses, and their body language. "Your history and your future are with you always," he said while holding up his animal figures to show me. "See, they all look different, but they're lifelike. I get my inspiration from the people I speak to."

When I offered him 30 fen to read my fortune, he brushed the money aside. "No, you're only a kid." Seeing my disappointment, he added, "I'll tell you a secret: people live different lives and the differences are their own doing. As for you," he looked me up and down, "you will never be settled so I can't make any predictions."

Only later did I realise that he had actually given me a prediction and it was spot-on.

That short trip in 1975 added a new dimension to my travel experiences. As well as pursuing the wonders of nature, I was beginning to look at how other people lived and review my own experience in a larger context. I saw lives of poverty and ignorance, and lives of wisdom and satisfaction. And I was becoming curious about what caused these lives to be different.

Unfortunately, my freedom to travel, along with my independent life, came to an end when I was sent to the countryside for re-education on 1 March 1976.

9

The Daunting "Vast Field"

In late 1975 an ailing Chairman Mao launched what was to be his last political campaign, "Stopping the Reversal of the Right Deviationists". This was his bid to protect the legacies of the Cultural Revolution, including the countryside re-education so that the city graduates could "accomplish great things in the vast field". As a result, most of those who graduated in 1975 left for the countryside in March 1976.

Before the campaign, the countryside re-education had been considerably reduced in scope. By 1972, senior high schools had reopened and factories had begun to recruit workers. Mao's "vast field" had come to be seen as a dumping ground. The new campaign stirred up discontent. Families began to look for exemptions. Many high-ranking military parents got their children into the army where they could work in propaganda teams or military hospitals as only the army took priority over a countryside relocation.

I could have been spared the "vast field" given that the disabled, an only child with sick parents, and sole household residents were exempt. But my father's case had just been overturned and he was about to resume his old engineering job in Beijing. He was among the hundreds of "rehabilitated" and urgently needed engineers and skilled workers of the Beijing Second Construction Company, due to be recalled during February to May 1976. My form teacher suggested that if my father could postpone his return until after the March re-education send-off date, I might be able to stay in Beijing.

I wrote to my father to put this suggestion to him and his furious reply was: "To avoid hardship, you'd have me eat sorghum bread for another three months! This is not merely a filial issue but a reflection of your political attitude. I'll be back in February in the first group and you must go to receive your very much needed re-education!"

I was angry, not with him but with myself. *You should have known by now how selfish your father is. Why did you beg him for mercy?* Meanwhile, I couldn't help but sneer at his big words about my political attitude. He was simply paying me back for my rejection of Old Mushroom. I put my name down for re-education.

I did not feel too bad about leaving Beijing since almost everyone was in the same boat. Only three of our class stayed in Beijing: Ling, because of her disability; the new girl, an only child whose parents were sickly; and my book-lender friend, because of the power of his father, the lieutenant-general. I comforted myself when I received my papers, thinking, *You're one of many going and we'll all be in this together.*

I am sure most of my classmates dealt with their anxieties in a similar way. During times of upheaval, people find security in being one of many. But I still felt terribly sad when the local registration officer removed my resident's papers from my family's Beijing resident registration booklet.

After a two-and-a-half hour journey by bus, we arrived at the Great Sun's Town commune, on the border of Beijing and Hebei provinces. The commune, which governed dozens of villages and a machinery factory, was to take about one hundred graduates. Everyone hoped to be assigned to the factory as it was in the town centre and had running water. It also offered fixed working hours, which wasn't the case with field work. A male official read out the names of those being assigned to the factory first, and our class was excited because one after another the names of students in our class were called out. But he stopped just before my name was called.

I was at a loss to know why but didn't dare ask. A classmate did it for me, "I think you missed one."

The officer replied: “I didn’t miss anyone, and remember who’s in charge here.”

As I watched my classmates being led into the courtyard of the factory, my mouth went dry and my heart started beating fast. They looked back at me in sympathy, and I waved, trying to squeeze a smile onto my face. The sense of security I had had that we were all in this together dissipated.

My name was called among the last group of nineteen who were going to the Village of Guests, four kilometres away, in a semi-mountainous area. We were jammed onto trailers attached to two small tractors and, after travelling twenty minutes over a bumpy country road, we arrived at the village.

My mind was working overtime in those twenty minutes. My initial fear and panic had died down since again I was one of many, but I couldn’t understand why I had been separated from my classmates. It couldn’t be my father’s political problem since he had been “rehabilitated”. I recalled Fourth Grandma’s words, “Everything is predestined.” I could only hope for the best.

“We’re here,” someone sitting up front announced. We craned our necks and some at the back tried to stand up to catch a glimpse of the Village of Guests.

The road became quite steep as we passed through the village entrance, flanked by two enormous Chinese scholar trees. As we got closer, we could see that the village was built on a slope and consisted of three parallel streets, which crossed the steep main road. The first cross street was called Lower Street, the second Middle Street and the third High Street.

As our tractors sputtered and jolted up the steep pot-holed road, we clung on to avoid being tossed out. Many villagers, men and women, old and young, hands inserted in their sleeves and swaying from foot to foot to keep warm, had lined up on the road to look at us. Children were running after the tractors, in between wandering dogs, chickens, ducks and geese.

It was a scene that was very foreign to us city youth. Fourth Grandma's village was nothing like this. Some of our group waved to the villagers but I, and many others, remained frozen, in shock.

The tractor stopped at the western end of High Street, in an open space by a big pond. Along one side of the open space was a row of brick terrace houses, the dormitory for the city graduates.

Around twenty older graduates, some of whom had been in the village for two years, were gathered there to welcome us. They had prepared a big pot of hot noodle soup with steamed buns as our welcome "banquet". Their smiling city faces and the steaming hot buns and soups they offered under a sunny blue sky calmed us down a bit. We jumped off the tractors and devoured the warm food. I joined in, talking and laughing with the others.

After the quick meal, we were led to brigade headquarters for our official reception. From the start of the re-education program, a myriad of articles, songs and published diaries had spoken of the warmth and kindness of the poor and lower-middle peasants, how they had made millions of city graduates feel they were coming home. Like the other graduates, I was therefore expecting a warm official welcome.

Headquarters consisted of two large rooms and a courtyard in the centre of Middle Street. The village co-op and the public toilets were also in the courtyard. We stood in the courtyard surrounded by a few dozen curious peasants listening to a speech by the village's director of the city graduates, a short man with bulging eyes called Jia. There was no warmth in Jia's face. He repeated the familiar official cant about the significance and necessity of city youngsters being re-educated but finished with the slogan, "No dishonest tricks, no unruly words and deeds, and strict obedience!"

This felt like one of the public denunciation meetings that I had attended at school and around the neighbourhood. The difference was that I now belonged to the denounced party. My feelings were obviously shared by my schoolmates. A general murmur arose among us.

Jia was annoyed. "Not happy about it? Okay, I'm going to give you your first instructions." He pulled a roll of paper from his jacket pocket, looked over each page then called out: "Wang Baoping, come forward, quick!"

A tall girl stood up and walked gingerly to the front. I knew her as the leader of our school choir. She also had a reputation for bourgeois tendencies because she liked to wear her mother's old embroidered shirts.

"You have a good voice, they say, but a bad attitude. All right, I'll give you a chance to redeem yourself. Come sing a song for our people."

Embarrassed, the girl could not produce a sound. Jia yelled, "You see, she refuses to sing for us, the revolutionary masses! This is a typical case of disobedience and deserves punishment. Go stand on the side."

Sobbing, Wang Baoping moved to the corner.

I felt very sorry for her. "Killing the chicken to frighten the monkey," was an old saying. I hoped not to become another chicken, and I have no doubt that the rest of the group had the same hope.

All of our personal files had been forwarded to the village and the tall girl's tears and our submissiveness went to Jia's head. The welcome meeting turned into a public denunciation. He called out more girls. Some had been caught going out with boys and some had broken school rules. Then my name was called.

"Take a good look at her," he said loudly as, head buried on my chest, I walked through the crowd to join the shamed team. "She seemed a good student at school but listen to this." He fetched a letter from his pocket and read: "My daughter tried hard to avoid this most wonderful re-education opportunity. She even tried to stop me from returning to Beijing to participate in revolutionary reconstruction. Please, comrades, make sure to nurture her and educate her thoroughly."

My father had written this letter! No wonder I had been singled out and sent here! Shocked and numb, I do not recall any other remarks Jia made about me as I stood there.

Reporting someone to the authorities during the Cultural Revolution could have gruesome consequences, even death for the person reported. Hadn't my father himself suffered terrible punishment because of a postman's report? To me, this felt like a betrayal.

I didn't hate my father, then or at any other time. The old values of respect for one's parents were deeply ingrained in me. But this incident made me decide to have nothing more to do with him, and heightened my innate distrust of people.

A village was considered a production brigade, and our brigade contained three production teams. I was assigned with seven other girls to the second production team. Because of the lack of beds in the graduates' dormitory, we were housed in an abandoned house behind brigade headquarters, which must have been vacant for some time because it smelled very stuffy. This was another setback. To me, the dormitory replicated city living but this place symbolised rural poverty and abandonment. I did my best not to break down into tears, as some of the girls had when the team leader, Baolin, showed us around the house.

It was a typical northern country house with three rooms in a row, side by side. The middle room functioned as both foyer and kitchen and the other two were bedrooms. Instead of beds, brick bases called *kang* were built along the front windows and took up half the room. The villagers slept on a *kang* with their feet pointing outwards, to the windows. Each *kang* had a hollow core that ran from one end to the other. One end was ducted to the brick cooking range in the middle room and the other end to a side chimney.

When villagers cooked with dry hay or firewood, the heat would flow under the *kang* and the smoke escape up the chimney. After a meal was cooked, the brick bed would be warm, allowing the villagers to sleep in comfort in winter. That first year, we graduates were not allowed to cook because we had not earned our own fuel, that is, sorghum stalks or hay, and the village could not spare us any. We ate our three meals in our designated kitchen near the main graduates' dormitory but our rooms were cold and our brick *kang* were icy. Fortunately, the *kang* in our small house was four metres (the length of the room) by two metres so the four of us could squeeze onto one *kang* and keep each other warm with our combined body heat.

After our long journey and dramatic "welcome", the other girls soon fell asleep, but I was wide awake. I was shaking like someone with malaria, not from the cold but from fear. While others who had been publicly named and shamed had cried uncontrollably after the meeting, I remained outwardly calm. I cleaned the middle room, swept the yard and helped the others arrange the sleeping quarters. But my mind was in turmoil.

From the day I was born, my family had endured one misfortune after another. I had lost my mother and seen my family scattered to the far reaches of the country. I had battled hunger, cold and loneliness, public scrutiny and accusations of criminal activity, accepting them as normal. To survive, I had learnt to live by certain principles: expect disappointment; believe in resilience and self-fulfilment; and seek no help, company, or approval from others. This had got me through adversity and I had imagined the worst was past!

Today's setbacks devastated me, and not only because my father had publicly humiliated and betrayed me. What cast me into despair was the thought that what he had done had sealed my fate here. Like every other graduate, my chance of eventually escaping country exile lay in the hands of the local authorities. That chance seemed to have been scuttled on day one.

The difference between the city and the country in China was huge. Before I left Beijing, I had heard a lot of talk about the primitive lives of the peasants: they did not brush their teeth, never showered, spat inside the house, and still practised arranged marriages. Women were not allowed to eat at the family table and were abused by their men. I had believed these claims to be greatly exaggerated, but in just half a day in the village I had seen enough to support them: the scruffiness of most of the villagers, the coarse language of the young, and the older women who had taken their tops off to delouse themselves in the sun during the meeting.

And the toilets! They were set in the corner of the yard, right next to the pigsties. Just after we arrived, one girl rushed into the toilet in the graduates' compound but dashed straight back out with her trousers around her knees, screaming, "Pigs! Two pigs bit me!"

There was more. When Baolin showed us around the empty house, his wife tagged along, ostensibly to help us settle into our new home. Her true purpose, however, was to satisfy her curiosity about city people. She looked through all our things without embarrassment, picked some sausages out of one girl's bag and made what appeared to be a joke about them. No one understood what she was getting at so she flipped through everyone's diaries – we all kept diaries to record our "daily revolutionary achievements" – until she found a photo of a young man in the diary of the tall girl, Wang Baoping. Pointing at it, she said excitedly, "You like him because of his sausage."

It was shocking to hear such language, yet what followed was more incredible: the team leader wheeled around and slapped her so hard that her nose started bleeding. Wang Baoping began to scream. The rest of us were speechless. While we rummaged through our medicine bag for cotton and gauze, the wife wiped her nose with her sleeve and yelled at her husband, "Shouldn't you wait until we get home to slap me? Don't scare the kids. They're our guests, sent by Chairman Mao."

If crushing elitist subversive elements was the aim of Mao's Cultural Revolution, the re-education policy served that purpose well. There is no doubt my schoolmates and I were bullied into subservience by Jia's intimidating reception and the austerity of village life.

That first night I stared into the dark as I had in the Buddhist Temple at Mount Emei, but instead of imagining Dantès escaping the dungeon, I now saw that emotionless mother in Fourth Grandma's village. I shivered violently, fearing that one day my life might become like hers and that of the team leader's wife.

*

The next morning, at daybreak, a loud clanging summoned us to a big tree in Middle Street. This was the daily routine in every Chinese village until 1984, when the commune system was disbanded. There would be a gong hanging on a tree – usually a piece of heavy metal – and the team leader would beat it, allowing fifteen minutes for his team to assemble under the tree. Our second production team comprised around a hundred labourers who squatted as they waited, looking sleepy and lifeless. There were also six boys who had arrived from Beijing the year before. They squatted like the other villagers.

We, the eight new arrivals, stood in a corner. Our team leader introduced us, telling the villagers to be kind but firm and to re-educate us in the best way they could. Then he began to assign the day's jobs – sowing sorghum in the north field, ploughing in the south field, collecting manure from the pigsties, and taking the horses to the vet in town. Certain jobs were considered worse than others, for example, the north field was three kilometres away, ploughing was hard labour, and manure collection was difficult and dirty. As a result, there was some muttering and shouting of "unfair" from the villagers. As newcomers, we said nothing; we didn't know what was fair and what was unfair.

People went home to wash and have breakfast before going to their assigned posts about an hour later. The day would not end until sunset, and in the country there was no weekend.

All eight of us were sent to the south field to follow the plough. As soon as the team leader made the announcement, the six boys, the older graduates, burst out laughing.

"What's wrong? Why are you laughing?" Ying asked them. We had elected Ying as the leader of our group of eight after the team leader and his wife left the very first day because she had been held up as an "advanced political exemplar" right through school.

"Well, following the plough is not a job for graduates. The team leader did exactly the same thing to us last year. It's what they call a 'head-on blow'," one boy replied.

"Well, we're here to be re-educated so we should welcome the 'head-on blow'," Ying responded, and led our frightened group away.

Each plough was pulled by a horse and managed by two people. A villager walked in front, controlling how fast and in which direction the horse walked while one of us followed behind, pressing the plough down to a certain depth in the soil. The field was rough and uneven, the ground was half-frozen, and we had neither the skill nor the strength to plough properly. We set the plough either too deep or too shallow and, despite the villager's best efforts to keep a steady pace, the plough would be stuck one moment and jolt forward the next.

Two of us took turns to follow each of the four ploughs. Without exception, we all fell: backwards, forwards, left and right. The field was about five hundred metres long and by the time we reached the other end, every one of us had injured ourselves. I had a bruised knee from a fall and chapped hands from the rough handle of the plough. Ying had come off the worst: she was missing a tooth. She had lost control of her plough handle, which bounced back and struck her in the face. We were almost in tears when we saw the blood streaming out of her mouth, but Ying wiped it off with her scarf and said, "We must show the right attitude. The whole point of having this re-education is to rid us of our squeamishness so we can be worthy heirs to the revolution."

Everyone was astonished by this, including the villagers. "We have a heroine here," someone called out, and others agreed. I echoed the cheers but thought I could never not be squeamish in this kind of setting. I comforted myself, *Anyway, with your bad origins, you'll never make it as a worthy daughter of the revolution, so you might as well just go on feeling squeamish.*

Promoting heroes was one of Mao's strategies. Throughout the Cultural Revolution, *The China Daily* regularly lionised exemplary figures. We had the model peasant Wang Guofu, who "lived in a poor house but cared about the whole world"; the model worker Ironman Wang Jinxi, whose only desire was to "share the concerns of the party and produce oil for the nation"; and the model soldier Mai Xiande, who fought against the invading Taiwanese despite a serious head injury. These heroes had two things in common: martyrdom and proletarian origins. They were Ying's inspiration. She believed Chairman Mao's every word and took all propaganda as gospel. I found her a bit over the top, as did many others, but I respected her because she always put her own interests last.

The villagers enjoyed watching us suffer. This "head-on blow" was our initiation – to put us in our place from day one. However, the villagers were fundamentally decent people, and after the lunch break they let us sit and watch. When Baolin arrived and began to scold us for loafing, the villagers told him off, "Look, they're just kids. Even our women don't do this shit job."

"I'm just carrying out Chairman Mao's orders," Baolin said in his defence. He then turned to us. "Okay, this afternoon, you can watch our poor and lower-middle peasants and learn some real skills."

In the following days, we took turns collecting manure. Every household had a pigsty and every month they would muck it out and pile the manure outside their house for the production team to collect in a horse-drawn cart and use as fertilizer on the fields. It was a job for two people, the driver and an assistant. We were the assistants for our team's three carts.

If following a plough was the hardest job, collecting manure was the dirtiest. In our village, every graduate was given these two jobs in the first week. Although shovelling the manure onto the cart and spreading it on the fields was not as hard as following the plough, the filth was unbearable and the smell nauseating. No matter how thoroughly we washed ourselves afterwards, the smell lingered for days.

We found the first week difficult. In addition to the hard labour, we suffered terribly from the cold, wintry weather. It was so cold that sometimes we would wake up with ice masks on our faces. All of our washing – face, body, clothes – was done with cold water, drawn from one of the three village wells. Scooping water out of a deep well with a bucket dangling from a long rope required skill; and carrying two buckets full of water on a shoulder pole needed strength and balance.

That week, every one of us endured the embarrassment of losing buckets in the well or spilling more than half the water on the way home. Everyone took turns crying at night except for Ying and me.

While Ying drew inspiration from the heroic deeds of revolutionary martyrs, I withdrew into myself, determined not to reveal my feelings. When my roommates asked me questions about my father's letter, I refused to answer. I was depressed and felt like giving up. My roommates tolerated my behaviour because what my father had done was extraordinary and they felt sorry for me.

To my surprise, the villagers felt sorry for me too. They didn't ask me questions, but wherever I appeared I would hear them whisper, "That's the girl who was condemned by her father." Then I would hear things like: "What a father – even beasts protect their young."

I felt that they meant me to hear their comments. There were many helping hands to fish my lost bucket out of the well and show me how to fill it with water, and then someone would demonstrate how to walk as you balanced a shoulder pole. These were strangers. They were my re-educators but they seemed to be less aware of class differences than my father, that "Rightist" and "active reactionary", was. They put me in mind of my neighbour Aunt Li, the chairman of the neighbourhood revolutionary committee in Beijing. I started to feel more positive about the peasants. I started to look beyond their shabby clothes and rough manner, and saw their kind hearts.

There was a 24-hour caretaker in brigade headquarters, a Mr Lieu, a man in his forties. Crippled by polio, he had to use crutches to get about – everyone called him Limper Lieu – and that was why he had been assigned to this job. He was the village receptionist who made tea for official guests; he also read the news, broadcast music and delivered messages over the PA system. His musical choices were very limited: during the entire two years I spent in the village, I heard no more than six songs. His announcements, however, were far more varied. For example:

"Tall Zhang of the first team had his first grandson, born at 2:00

am this morning and weighing 3.3 kilograms."

"Dwarf Yang of the second team: your father-in-law has come to visit, please return home immediately."

"Widower Zhao's cat had a litter of eight; if anyone wants a mouse catcher, please let him know."

The postman came once a week to deliver and collect mail. When he announced that the postman for the commune of Great Sun's Town would be arriving around lunchtime the next day, every homesick graduate spent the night writing letters and trying to guess what they were going to receive from home.

I did not write to my father or any of my brothers, nor did I expect to receive anything from my family. I was feeling a great deal of resentment towards the family I had been born into. Why did I always have to endure these ridiculous twists and turns?

The next day when all the graduates rushed to headquarters after work, I stayed in the dormitory. They soon returned, some cheerfully waving letters or showing off food parcels. others empty-handed and dispirited. I did not want to be involved in their conversations so I picked up the buckets to go and fetch water from the well. Suddenly the PA system was switched on and Limper Lieu was shouting: "Xiyan of the second team, please come to headquarters immediately."

I stopped at the gate, wondering if I had heard correctly. Lieu's voice rose again as Ying dashed out to tell me that I was being called. "Go, go. I'm sure it'll be a nice letter. I'll get the water." She was kind but she had no idea what my family was like. Reluctantly, I walked to headquarters.

Limper Lieu looked me up and down. "Why didn't you come to collect your letter?"

"I didn't think I'd have one."

"Such a cold-hearted girl." He picked up a letter from his desk. I saw my father's unmistakable handwriting on an official envelope of Beijing Second Construction Company. He had just regained his senior engineer's position in the company and clearly wanted to let everybody know it. My first impulse was to refuse to take it but I said, "Thank you," to Limper Lieu, took the letter and turned towards the door.

"Wait! You think I called you just for this letter?" He blocked the door with his crutches. "I have a message for you. Go to High Street, No. 19, and call on Immortal Zheng. He saw the envelope and said he knew your family. Make sure you go tonight because I don't want to offend him."

"Who is this Immortal Zheng?" I asked in disbelief. "How can someone in this village know my family?"

"Well, Immortal Zheng is not just 'someone'. Go read the letter and visit him." He moved his crutches out of the way to let me out.

My father's letter was full of official jargon. In the "vast field", he instructed me, I should observe more, listen more, do more but say less so that I would one day be truly re-educated. He warned me to be careful in my choice of friends in a new place and copied in one of Chairmen Mao's quotations: "People everywhere are divided into left, middle and right by their ideologies."

He did not mention the letter he had sent to the commune leaders but at the end asked me to remember that only those who loved us could speak words unpleasant to hear. His meaning was clear – he felt he had been justified in writing that letter. His words filled me with contempt: *If you are so wise, why have you brought so much trouble to my mother and our family?*

Nevertheless, his admonition about imprudent friendships stopped me going to see Immortal Zheng that day. Perhaps my father issued this warning because he had known this Immortal Zheng would contact me? The last thing I needed was to be associated with a bad element. His title, Immortal, sounded suspicious in the context of the Cultural Revolution.

The following day I was working with a group of women sowing corn seed. The field had been ploughed into regular furrows and we sowed in pairs, one in front dropping the seeds into the furrow, the other covering the seeds with soil. I was paired with a quiet woman who frequently stopped to wait for me and sometimes helped me. I felt it was safe to ask her who this Immortal Zheng was. As soon as his name was mentioned, her quiet manner fell away.

"Immortal Zheng? He's the man I dreamed of marrying," she exclaimed loudly.

"How dare you? It wouldn't have been your turn," another woman chimed in. "I had that dream much before you."

More women joined in:

"Oh, I only want some of his luck."

"Me too. Let's poison his wife and then we can share – "

The last woman was cut short by the group leader, Baolin's wife. "Shut up! If you don't shut up, I'll tell my husband and get him to assign you all to the north field tomorrow!"

Later my partner told me that Immortal Zheng was Baolin's brother, the brother-in-law of Baolin's wife.

I couldn't get much sense out of these women, but I concluded that a visit to this mysterious man would be safe. The brother of our team leader would not be a class enemy. I was not keen on the visit but I didn't want to risk offending "the poor and lower-middle peasants" by refusing their invitation.

10

The Village of Guests

I took a deep breath and pushed open the double timber doors of No. 19 High Street. The noise of the rusty door hinge startled me. Stopping inside the dark gateway, I took another deep breath and walked into a big yard lined with trees. It was dusk and two little girls were feeding a large flock of hens. When they saw me, they dropped the feed and ran into the house. A tall woman walked out and said, "Is that you, Xiyan? We've been waiting for you since yesterday. Come in please."

As I stepped into the middle room, a man lifted the quilted curtain from inside the west wing: "Xiyan, welcome! Come here quickly. It's too cold out there."

I couldn't see a face clearly but I felt a warmth, a long-missed family warmth. I relaxed a bit and entered the brightly lit west wing.

I had already been to quite a few homes – thanks to our initiation into manure collection. It was the local custom that after we loaded the manure onto the cart, we were invited in to wash our hands and have a cup of tea.

In a typical northern villager's home, the principal room was in the west wing, the east wing being divided into sections such as the children's bedroom and the storeroom. Half of the principal room was taken up by a big brick *kang*. Most west wings were quite large, about seven metres by five and the *kang* would be 7 metres by 2.5 metres. During the day, quilts and bedding were neatly folded and piled at the warm end of the *kang*, next to the middle room where the cooking ranges were, while the other end of the *kang* – always covered with a bamboo mat – became the "living room". A low table would be set on it and tea and meals were served there. Opposite the *kang* would be a sideboard, a table and a few chairs. The wall behind these was normally covered with family photos, certificates, and pretty cut-outs from colour magazines.

There were some exceptional features in Immortal Zheng's west wing: it had a stove in the middle of the room for heating, and an antique sideboard along the wall with a big grandfather clock next to it. The room had a cultivated look. The biggest difference, though, was in what was on the wall. Instead of the usual messy displays, there were two large framed pictures. One was a collage of family memorabilia and the other was a photograph of a young man seated on a chair playing an *erhu* with a woman in her forties standing beside him, singing. I froze when I caught sight of the photo, then stepped closer to get a better look.

"Yes, it's your mother, Big Sister Yukang," I heard Zheng say behind me.

I had not expected the connection to be with my late mother. I turned to face him in stunned silence. He was in his mid-forties, of a tall and slim build, and with a kind face. He sat me down and took the photograph out of the frame. On the back was written: "Parting souvenir to Little Brother Baochang – I wish you every success in the vast field!" It was my mother's handwriting and her signature. The date was May 1956. Seeing her familiar handwriting after everything that had happened, I couldn't hold back my tears.

Zheng's wife came in with a warm towel. "Don't cry. It's okay. Come, wipe your tears." She was a pretty woman and her smiling face was radiant. "Sit down and have some tea, dinner will be ready soon." As she spoke, the two little girls brought in a pot of newly made tea and poured it into two cups, one for their dad and one for me.

Zheng introduced their daughters as twelve-year-old Poplar and ten-year-old Willow. They said hello shyly and left the room.

Over the pot of tea, I learnt about Immortal Zheng – Baochang was his given name – and his association with my mother. As the clever son of the family, he had been sent to study in a Beijing high school. After graduation, his musical talent had earned him a job in the workers' union of Beijing Second Construction Company. My mother was one of the union leaders at the time and her job was to organise entertainment for the workers.

For more than two years, Baochang had performed for the workers busily building the Ten Grand Constructions in preparation for the ten-year anniversary of New China. Then in 1956, the government called on the educated young people who had been born in rural areas to return home to help with the commune movement, so he left Beijing. My mother gave him the photo as a parting gift.

"At first I didn't like country life and felt lost. You must be feeling the same." Seeing me nod, he continued, "You know what made me change? Your mother's letters. She wrote me many letters persuading me to accept reality and telling me an empty life was not worth living. So I settled down and I'm very content now.

"I've never forgotten her, Big Sister Yukang – that's what we called her. She was caring, loving and full of energy. Working with her was fun. Often after a late rehearsal, she'd take our group of young single workers to a restaurant for dinner. We did not fear her; we all respected her. But a few years later, she stopped replying to my letters. I heard about your father's case and her forced resignation. That's how come we lost contact. When I saw the company's envelope and your father's name, I was so happy at the thought of seeing her again."

I told Baochang that my mother had died more than three years ago and that this night's encounter had made me realise how little I knew about her.

This saddened Baochang. "Oh, she died too young. You were so little when she died. How could you have known her well?"

He called his wife and daughters in and announced: "From now on, Xiyan is a member of our family. When we have one mouthful of good food, she'll have half. When she gets married, we'll make the wedding quilts for her, our daughter."

"Of course!" his wife echoed. She turned to the girls. "Hear that? Xiyan is your big sister."

The family of four smiled but I cried, out of gratitude and joy. Wedding quilts were traditionally an essential dowry for a girl. Her mother needed to sew four new cotton-filled quilts for the wedding chamber to guarantee the girl's future happiness.

After being denounced by my own father, I had been at my lowest point emotionally, but suddenly here was a new family unconditionally embracing me. It was like a dream so I kept cautioning myself: *Don't be too excited. Tomorrow may be different. Just be happy that you've had such a pleasant evening.*

The dinner was delicious crispy pancakes filled with cabbage, scrambled eggs mixed with young chives, and deep-fried meat-filled dumplings. This was food you would normally only find in a city kitchen. We also drank spirits, and when I was relaxed by the alcohol I asked him why the villagers called him Immortal Zheng. He laughed. "People think I'm protected by someone in Heaven."

Apparently, his luck had never run out. He had married the most beautiful woman in the region; their son was tall, handsome, worked at the commune department store and received a monthly salary while other peasants were subsistence farmers with scarcely any cash to show for their labour. The Immortal himself was not a robust farm labourer, but everything he touched turned out to be the best.

Under the commune system, individual peasants did not own land but every year each family was given a private lot of one-fifth of an acre for growing their own vegetables, peanuts and any other special food. To avoid arguments, the villagers would draw lots after Spring Festival to see who got which plot of land. Whichever piece of land the Immortal drew, what it produced would be the most abundant and of the best quality. One year his jealous younger brother, the team leader, swapped their lots after the draw. The land may have been swapped but luck stayed with the Immortal.

In their private yards, villagers were also allowed to have chickens, goats and pigs to make extra cash, and fruit trees for bartering articles for everyday use. His pigs were the fattest, his hens laid eggs twice a day and his apricots and peaches were the envy of everyone. It was not surprising he became known as Immortal Zheng.

I couldn't sleep for excitement. How could I be so lucky as to land in this Village of Guests and meet the Immortal?

The Cultural Revolution called on us to "Break with the Four Olds: old ideas, old culture, old customs, and old habits." However, so deep was the tradition of ancestor worship that the belief in life after death could not be eradicated. I was a true believer in the afterlife because Fourth Grandma had filled my head with many stories involving ghosts: how a mother's ghost saved her daughter from being poisoned by her adulterous husband; how a father's spirit attached itself to his sleepwalking son to prevent him from falling off a cliff. And so that night I wondered if my mother's spirit had had something to do with this unexpected meeting. Why, after I had been condemned by the village authorities, did her old friend appear and save me? Why, when I was about to give up, did her words – "an empty life is not worth living" – echo?

There were holes in my theory. If someone had facilitated the encounter with Immortal Zheng, that someone should have been my father. It was his first letter that had condemned me to this village and brought me "renown", and it was his second letter that had brought me to Baochang's attention. Nevertheless, I preferred not to follow that line of reasoning.

It was a beautiful night and a real turning point in my life. I had been sinking, but now felt myself surfacing again with the love and support of my new family. I emerged from my isolation!

The Village of Guests, formerly Qie, was located midway on the route between the plains region to the south and Twenty Mile Long Mountain region to the north. During the Qing dynasty, a certain Charitable Li had opened an inn in the village, offering travellers a meal and a bed free of charge. After he died, his children turned the inn into a business and many other villagers followed suit. The village had thus functioned as a midway resting place, become famous for its warmth to strangers and its fine cooking, and earned its current name, The Village of Guests.

We newcomers soon found that the village still deserved its reputation, despite Mr Jia and the one or two other village leaders who had been carrying out Mao's instructions regarding re-educating us. Very few in the village shared their mean and hostile attitude, and within a month nearly every one of the new arrivals had been invited to villagers' homes for food and drinks.

Normally the villagers ate simple meals, but if they had a visitor or it was a family occasion – a birthday, a married daughter returning home, etc. – they would prepare a delicious banquet. Whenever this happened, they would remember us, the "poor homeless city kids", and either invite a couple of us to their banquet or bring leftovers to the field the next day. According to the older graduates, this tradition dated back to 1972 when the first group arrived at the Village of Guests.

Most of the villagers had never been to Beijing or any other city. As well as showing hospitality, they were keen to learn more about the outside world, represented for them by the nation's capital.

Immortal Zheng enjoyed great popularity in the village, and it was through him that I became acquainted with many of the villagers. One night, at his suggestion, the former leader of our second production team invited me, along with my seven roommates, to his sixtieth birthday banquet. After a few drinks, people began to fire questions at us: "How did city people eat – sitting at a table or squatting on the kitchen floor?" "Why did Tiananmen Square have to be so big? You could have harvested several hundred kilos of wheat there."

Our team's deputy party secretary, a young man with a reputation for cleverness, asked a serious question about the traffic lights: "I know when the lights change from red to green, cars and bicycles can go. But I've been wondering for a long time how the lights get changed. Does a policeman switch them on and off from under the road? What if he falls asleep?"

"Indeed," the birthday man added, with the certainty of a village elder, "even if he was slack for a single moment, there could be an accident. I'd never let my son take a job like that – too stressful."

We walked back to our dormitory. Because many other guests had left at the same time and were walking near us, we tried hard to contain our laughter. As soon as we got inside, we rolled about on the *kang*, nearly splitting our sides laughing at their "ignorance". But afterwards, Ying asked how *did* the lights get changed, and no one knew. Then we laughed again, this time at ourselves.

The eight of us had become very close after living together for a couple of months, separated from the main group of graduates. When the winter chill had gone, we also appreciated our relative isolation. We felt much freer to talk or laugh because all the official attention was directed at the main dormitory. Immortal Zheng had given our group many opportunities to associate with the locals, which not only meant good meals and a break from routine, but also the honour of being accepted by the poor and lower-middle peasants. My roommates regarded my connection to Immortal Zheng as luck we shared, and they were grateful to me. I had changed a lot, feeling more relaxed, more trusting of people. I enjoyed living with other girls, the chats, the fun, the laughter and, occasionally, a good cry.

The village was a close-knit community bound by ties of blood and marriage. They helped one another build houses, landscape yards, and organise weddings and funerals. All this took place after work or during the long lunch breaks in the hot season. There were also banquets for thanking the helpers. At first, we graduates enjoyed only the banquets, if we were invited, but gradually some of us began to join the teams of helpers.

I pitched in to help our team leader, Baolin, Immortal Zheng's brother, put a mud roof on his new storeroom. The family had prepared the clay mud and mixed it with hay before the helpers arrived. Two or three experienced roofers stood on top of the roof frame and the others down below picked up balls of mud around twenty centimetres in diameter and heaved them up to the roofers, who quickly flattened them in neat rows like fish scales.

It was not easy to be a mud thrower: the clay was heavy. But as a representative of Immortal Zheng's family I was determined not to lose face for the family, so I kept throwing and throwing until lunch arrived. I was given a big bowl of rice with a huge topping of braised pork. My arms were so sore I could hardly pick the bowl up.

The villagers were impressed by my hard work and started calling on me frequently to help, which made me feel special. I followed a cart collecting rocks for someone's new pigsty; I made bricks during lunch breaks for a wheat barn; I marched a roof beam around the village in a house-building ritual; and I registered the guests and gifts for birth celebrations, weddings and a funeral. Within six months, I had become the most invited graduate in the village. In that labour-intensive community, invitations came for a capable pair of hands so I took this as validation of my abilities. I enjoyed countless banquets and learnt a lot about rural life.

One time, I did the registration job for the wedding of Mr Zhang of the third team. It was very different from the weddings in Beijing where families and friends would gather in a wedding chamber decorated with a few red paper-cuttings of the double-happiness character, 囍. There, the gifts were mostly the four volumes of Chairman Mao's complete works or various portraits of him. Sometimes there might be a face basin or a thermos bottle from the closest relatives. The guests would sit and chat, eat roasted peanuts and candies for an hour or so, and that was it.

At Zhang's house, however, they sat me down behind a small desk at the gate. Every guest had to register and leave their gift with me before entering the yard. Another helper would open the gift and announce loudly what it was so I could record it next to the guest's name. A third person then came to take the gift inside.

There were more than fifty guests and a great variety of gifts. As well as bed sheets, pillow cases, dressing mirrors, toilet articles, plates and bowls, there was a gigantic rabbit cage, a big roll of chicken wire, a wooden trunk, a tiny needle and thread box, embroidered shoe soles and cotton socks. When I finished the last registration and went in to join the wedding banquet, I was amazed to see all the gifts already on display. Bedding had been hung on the lines around the yard like flags of all nations, small gifts were piled on a huge table in the middle, and surrounding the table were the bigger gifts. I had entered an exhibition centre. Apparently the grander the exhibition, the prouder the host would be. This was another way of indicating the level of respect a family was accorded in the community.

Eight tables had been set up in the front yard with cheerful people gathered around them. A professional chef had been engaged to churn out all kinds of dishes in a temporary outdoor kitchen from which delicious aromas wafted. The contrast of the brilliant white buns with the vibrant colours of the dishes was incredibly beautiful. The banquet started at noon and lasted till sunset and the mood was joyous.

The wedding took place in the middle of September. By then, the busy harvest season was nearly over. The village had delivered their grain quota to the state, and individual families had brought in their own produce from their private lots. People were able to take time off during this last warm month and organise weddings and engagements, or visit relatives. Their granaries were full, their kitchen ranges busy and their spirits high. This was the happiest month of the year, when people could indulge themselves a bit.

It was during that month that I was invited to be a judge in a matchmaking event for the son of a Mr Li.

All marriages in the village were arranged by parents or village elders, but began with a matchmaker's proposal. If there was nothing inappropriate in the background of the family making the proposal then it would be followed by financial negotiations. The woman's family would present their dowry list, and the man's family would build the bridal chamber and pay for the wedding banquet. When all this was settled, there would be the final judgment – the third stage. The young man, his parents and their three judges would visit the young woman's family and meet their three judges. To my knowledge, the three judges were usually an elder, a "knowledgeable" person and one of the family's best friends. No formal questions were asked. Instead, the judges would observe the other party's words and deeds throughout the banquet. Afterwards, they expressed their concerns:

"The young man appeared to be a bit greedy when he was eating. You must make sure they have enough food on the table."

"A button fell off the jacket of the young woman's father. You should ask around to see if her mother is lazy. You don't want your daughter-in-law to spend half her time looking after her own family."

So when the Li family called on me, I thought they had made a mistake.

"No, we do want to invite you, because you're from Beijing and very knowledgeable. You know what kind of girl our family needs."

I was thrilled to be given this most honourable role and to be regarded as an insider. My re-education had clearly gone well; perhaps the local authorities would be pleased with me and eventually allow me to return to the city.

Arranged marriages was one of the worst of the rural traditions. Although the Communist Party had campaigned ever since it took power in 1949 in favour of freedom to choose your marriage partner, it was still regarded in the 1970s as flippant and immoral, and often condemned in villages. The only new element allowed in rural communities was that the future bride and groom could meet in person before the marriage was sealed, during the judgment day. That was usually at a very late stage and was a mere formality.

Fortunately, the matchmaking event I was involved in was an agreeable one. The future bride smiled shyly throughout the meeting and the future groom glowed with happiness. Both families were pleasant and everyone was very civil, leaving the two other judges on our side with nothing to be concerned about. When the Li family asked my opinion, I said, "Your son clearly likes her and she likes him. And most importantly, everyone in her family is good-looking so your grandchild will be handsome." They were all very impressed by my remark about the future grandchild who, under the newly introduced birth control policy, would be an only child and precious to the family.

Arranging a marriage for a sick or less capable man was cruel because village life was labour-intensive. A weak young man would be considered useless, reducing his value in the marriage stakes. Usually two options would be presented to his family. He could give up his surname and marry into his future wife's family. In this way her family, if it was one without a son, could ensure the family's surname was perpetuated. Or he could marry a bad-looking or a disabled girl.

Marriage arrangements were worst for the sister of a sick or disabled young man, because she became a bargaining chip for her brother. She was made to marry a member of her future sister-in-law's family – a brother or a cousin – no matter what kind of man he might be. This was called "exchange of daughters". Without an available sister, such a young man had much less chance of finding a wife.

One day when I went to headquarters to pick up the post, I met Limper Lieu's cousin – another polio victim who also relied on crutches. He had come to pick up a parcel for his wife. After he left, Limper Lieu said resentfully, "See, that is what we call fate. My cousin not only limps, he has pockmarks all over his face, but he has a beautiful wife and I'm a bachelor. Do you know why? Because he has a sister! Unfortunately I'm an only child." Then he explained the exchange business to me. I couldn't believe such a backward practice still persisted in the middle of the Cultural Revolution. I didn't share Limper Lieu's sentiments at all; instead, I was pleased that he didn't have a sister.

I became more aware of the different marriage arrangements in the village through my friendship with two young villagers: Feng and Bing. Each told me about their frustrations.

Feng was the leader of our second team's "Iron Girls"; this was a term that was fashionable during the Cultural Revolution for a group of young women who were as capable as men at working in the fields. At harvest time, Feng oversaw the maintenance of our team's temporary threshing ground, a piece of flat land topped with a layer of smooth clay mud mixed with hay. Both Bing and I were working under her supervision.

The villagers called the harvest "grabbing food from the dragon's mouth" because there was usually only a week of dry weather from the day they started harvesting to the day everything was bagged. People worked day and night during this week. Every afternoon, the crops would be laid out on the threshing ground. Then, while the villagers went home to have dinner, the electrician and the team leader would set up various machines – maize shellers, sorghum/rice threshers, and different sized air-blowers – and hook up large flood lights. After dinner, the nightly threshing would begin.

The young and strong worked at the machines, feeding ears of corn or rice in at one end, and removing the kernels of corn or grains of rice, along with the corncobs and rice straw, at the other end. The same procedure would be repeated with the air-blowers for sifting the grain. The old and feeble would sit in a circle and shell the remains of the kernels and grain by hand – nothing could be wasted. Other labourers would be busy moving corn or rice from machine to machine, sweeping the threshing ground and bagging the sifted grain. It looked like a battlefield with people racing in every direction as the team leader yelled commands over the roar of the machines, all the while dust from the husks filling the air.

I would have loved to operate a thresher but for safety reasons our team leader wouldn't allow graduates to touch the machines. So I was the ground sweeper who had to clear one kind of grain from the ground before a second kind arrived. This was important since rice, corn or sorghum had to be kept separate. The job required swift hands.

No one was allowed to go home until the threshing ground was empty, the grains bagged, straw and stalks bundled up, and everything moved to our team's warehouse. It was usually midnight by then. The next morning everyone was out in the field again by sunrise.

While others were out in the field, Feng would make sure we repaired the threshing ground, as a smooth and solid surface was very important for minimising grain loss. First, we went to the foot of the mountain behind the village to each collect a wheelbarrow of clay soil, which we then spread over the ground with some hay. Next, we began our repair work, section by section. Some of us watered the clay, others trod on it with bare feet to break up the lumps and mix the mud and hay evenly, and a third group ran the stone rollers – metre-long cylinders with thick ropes threaded through the middle – over the surface.

There was no running water so water had to be carried on shoulder poles from the village well. All the animals were being used in the fields, so the stone rollers had to be pulled by hand, in our case by two girls. We had to finish the repair job by early afternoon to allow time for the sun to dry the ground. We often had no lunch break until two or three o'clock.

I was the only graduate chosen to work in Feng's team because by then I could cart two full buckets of water in perfect balance. I was also strong enough to carry hundreds of buckets a day. However, I was not the only "only" figure. To my surprise, there was a young man – Bing – among the "Iron Girls". When I asked why he was in our team, the village girls laughed and began to tease him.

"Our Beijing guest wants to know why you're with us. What do you want us to say?"

Bing's face turned red.

"Should we say it's because you're an intellectual?"

"Or because you're going to marry a ghost woman?"

"Or simply, that you're not a man –"

Feng snapped, "Shut up, will you? Where are your hearts? Eaten by beasts?"

Bing was a slight, fine-featured young man in his early twenties.

During all this banter he bowed his head and said nothing. Feng ordered me to work with him. "Look, he's been bullied by the men so he's working with us. You're an educated person. I trust you to be nice to him."

Bing was not strong but he tried hard to keep up with everyone. He and I never failed in our water supply duties during that week. I liked Bing's gentle manner and Feng's fair and considerate leadership. By the time harvest was done, we three were friends and trusted one another.

In October, I was working with Feng's group again, irrigating the winter wheat field. This would be the last of the demanding field work to be done before the cold weather set in. The job had to be done at night to prevent the water from evaporating. We did it field by field, building up the ridges to retain the water, following the flow and removing any obstacles in its course, and then waiting half an hour for the water to seep in before we moved to another field. It was during those waiting periods that Feng and Bing opened up to me.

Bing was the third son of our retired team leader. He was more than ten years younger than his siblings so his parents had spoiled him and shielded him from hard labour. He was smart at school, but hopeless in the fields. So he was teased by the villagers as "a common rooster pretending to be a phoenix". He had such a bad reputation that matchmakers had warned his parents that no proper girl would want to marry their no-hoper son. Bowing to this criticism, not only had his father stopped him from completing senior high school, he had found him a future wife whose face was covered with the white patches of vitiligo. "At least your children will bear our family name!" his father had comforted him.

Bing was devastated. "I envy you city people. I just want to study. I really enjoy reading books," he said to me.

I felt sorry for him. I knew how he felt. I had been missing the pleasure of books since I left Beijing.

Feng was a good-looking woman with huge eyes and curly hair, but she was locked into a marriage exchange. Her brother, an only son, had speech problems, which prevented him from making a good match. In order to preserve a healthy family line, Feng's parents had promised one family that if they agreed to their daughter marrying Feng's brother then they would marry Feng off to their daughter's brother, who had a cleft palate. This deal had been made two years earlier and now the families were discussing the date for the double wedding. Feng was as depressed about her forthcoming marriage as Bing was about his.

I was angry that they had meekly accepted their fate. I rejected their defence that I didn't understand country life and urged them to fight against these backward customs and take control of their own lives. During my home break, I decided to save them from their tragic fate.

Every year, we graduates were granted three breaks, three days in June after the summer wheat harvest, one week at the end of September after the autumn harvest and two and a half weeks in January or February during Chinese New Year. My first break home was nothing exciting. Both my father and Dong were living at home by then and the house I had once lived in on my own felt crowded. The June break was short, and even though I enjoyed Dong's cooking, I spent most of those three days catching up on sleep in a proper bed.

My relationship with my father deteriorated further during this visit. We had avoided long conversations so initially were getting on peacefully. But on the day I was to leave, I had to ask him for 3.4 yuan for the bus ticket. I had not seen the 5 yuan note he had left on the dining table. He looked shocked and then said in a resigned voice, "Okay, I didn't know you'd sunk so low. You think I'm old so you can trick me." I was dumbfounded and hurt. Then he saw the money still on the table and realised he had accused me wrongly. He gave me the note but made no apology. Observing traditional filial obedience, I didn't say a word or express any grievance, but I didn't feel sorry to be returning to the village.

The autumn break was different. I had received my first annual remuneration – in addition to the provision of food for the following year, I had earned 97 yuan. This amount was decided by how many work points I had earned during those seven months. Most graduates received between 50 and 100 yuan so my earnings were near the top. This was extremely poor pay for more than seven months of hard labour, but I was thrilled because I had never seen such a big amount and I was free to control my money again. I kept 60 yuan as pocket money for the following year – no more begging from my father – and spent the rest. I had a reunion banquet with my classmates, a visit to my school, a picnic with Dong in the Summer Palace and I went shopping. I almost felt like I was on holiday, except of course I would have preferred to be continuing my travel adventures.

While at my old school, I collected a set of high school textbooks for Bing from our teachers. He could do something he enjoyed, read, in his free time. During the reunion I learnt from my classmates that the commune factory was about to recruit new workers from local villages, so I told them about Feng and asked them to help. Although I knew that the decision was not up to them, it might just work if all twenty city graduates who worked in the factory mentioned Feng's name.

I gave the textbooks to an excited Bing when I returned to the village and urged Feng to apply for the factory job. I also asked Immortal Zheng to speak to his brother, our team leader, on Feng's behalf. He did, but reminded me of an old saying: "People's fates are decided by heaven." In other words, what I did might change nothing.

Well-loved and highly capable as she was, Feng did get one of the jobs in the factory. My advocacy might have helped. It was a great honour for a village family for one of their own to become a salary earner. Feng's father agreed to postpone the double wedding.

I gave little thought to the warnings of Immortal Zheng and to the consequences of my actions, so intoxicated was I with feeling so self-satisfied and with the gratitude of Feng, Bing and other villagers. It would be a long time before I learnt that my "great help" had actually added misery to their lives.

11
A Happy Outsider

Going into winter there was little to do in the fields, so the commune's defence department decided to organise military training for the graduates. We had already had numerous bouts of military training at school. We had gone on long marches, and had learnt to crawl forward and climb posts, but this time the training involved live ammunition. We were to learn how to shoot semi-automatic rifles and hurl hand grenades. Like many others I was excited but, at the same time, scared. What if something went wrong?

Our training site was a vast plain four kilometres northwest of the village at the foot of Twenty Mile Long Mountain. Our trainer, Monitor Wang, was from a nearby army camp. Jia introduced him as experienced in training recruits. When he arrived at our training site in a big jeep, my fear gave way to enthusiasm. It was a sunny morning and the sight of a fully armed soldier in a gleaming car set against the backdrop of the mountains excited me.

Monitor Wang ordered us to set up ten targets and dig a long shallow trench about one hundred metres in front of the targets. He then commanded all thirty-nine of us to lie on our stomachs in the trench, lifting our heads to look at the targets while he worked his way along the trench checking our posture one by one: left arm tucked into the chest, right arm stretched out ahead to hold the imaginary gun steady; right leg bent and left leg straight so we would be ready to leap up and rush forward after shooting the enemy. Finally satisfied, he said, "Okay. You're ready." He marched back to his jeep and brought out a bunch of large trimmed tree branches. "Now hold these like a gun."

After two hours we were still holding branches. I had had enough and refused to pick up the branch. I wanted to be trained with real weapons. Others felt the same and some boys threw their branches away.

"Give us a real gun!" one boy demanded.

"We're not children. We're people's militia," another added.

Even Ying showed some attitude by dropping the branch she had accepted earlier.

Monitor Wang's face turned red. He thought for a while and then said, "Okay, I'll give you guns. But you must listen to my instructions very carefully and obey me at all times."

When he returned to the jeep to get the rifles, one girl voiced our thoughts when she commented, "I don't think he's experienced at all. I think he's nervous."

The semi-automatic rifles were very heavy. As soon as they were in our hands Monitor Wang clearly became agitated. "Hit the ground!" he yelled, so loudly that we obeyed at once. The mood changed and my earlier fear came back. Once again he checked our posture and made sure we were holding the guns properly, particularly that the butt was wedged tight against our right shoulder. "Otherwise you'll be badly hit by the recoil," he explained.

Ten at a time, we took turns to shoot. After each round, he ordered us to place the guns on the ground while he went to check the targets. More than half of us missed the target completely. I didn't miss but I only hit the three-point ring.

Because of Monitor Wang's endless checking and double-checking, by the end of the day we had only managed to have two shots each. According to the rules, you had to shoot ten times before you could advance to throwing hand grenades. On the way back to the village, some of the graduates moaned about our bad luck in scoring such a timid trainer. We had heard that the training in other villages was much quicker. "We might never get to see a hand grenade," one boy commented.

The boy was proved right, we didn't get the chance to see a grenade.

In fact, the shooting only lasted two days before the training suddenly stopped altogether. Within days, accident reports were being filed one after another. In one village, a girl had accidentally shot the trainer in the leg while he was checking the target; in another, a boy who had failed to hold his rifle snugly against his shoulder suffered a broken jaw. The worst case was a girl who hurled a grenade backwards, right into her group. The heroic trainer had thrown himself on the grenade to save everyone else, but he had been killed instantly. We realised then how lucky we had been to have had Monitor Wang.

These reports together with all kinds of wild rumours aroused great anxiety among us graduates. Some powerful parents threatened to report the commune to the Beijing government if they could not guarantee our safety. Under pressure, the commune leader decided to replace the live-ammunition training with general knowledge training. This decision led to my getting a special job.

My fourth-oldest brother, Dong, had taught me to draw and I had won second prize in my primary school art competition. During my years in high school my works had decorated the school bulletin board. This information was in my personal file. After the commune leader's decision to change our training, I was summoned to town, where the head of the commune's defence department asked me to draw weapons on big posters to be used in the general knowledge training. I was proud of being given this honour but worried it could prove dangerous if I made mistakes. I was put up in the town's guesthouse for three days to complete the drawings and luckily my work met the expectations of the authorities.

To my pleasant surprise, my drawing skills began to bring me benefits. The villagers were used to having their furniture decorated with traditional patterns or figures. In the old days, a craft shop in a region would have done this sort of work, but these shops had been abolished during the Cultural Revolution, even though the demand was still there. Once people heard that I could draw, invitations flowed, giving me entree into many villagers' homes. On a wardrobe

I drew a cabbage with crickets on it, on a trunk I drew a fat baby with a giant pumpkin, on a bedhead I drew a dragon and a phoenix and on a desk I drew flowers. Some women also asked me to draw embroidery patterns on their pillowcases and bed sheets. All of this should have been "illegal", but no one in the village seemed to care. I felt safe because many village leaders became my clients. To thank me they offered me eggs, sweet potato, grain coupons and meals.

In winter, we still went to work every day, but it was mainly to do maintenance: levelling the fields to ready them for the spring ploughing and sowing, looking after the over-used animals, or building small dams. However, we would start late and finish early so by four in the afternoon I would be in one of the villagers' homes drawing or engraving and would stay there till late. Because of this, I hardly ate dinner in the graduates' canteen at all during those cold months.

Through drawing, I also made more friends among the villagers. Mingcheng was one of these. I learnt how Mao's Cultural Revolution had affected his life and what a near miss I had had in not ending up like him.

Mingcheng was in his early thirties. He had the villagers' dark sun-scorched skin and was a group leader, but he had the aura and manner of a city person. He was also the only person who did not bear one of the four surnames – Jia, Zheng, Li and Zhang – common to the Village of the Guests. The village men liked to tease or flirt with us city girls, but Mingcheng was polite and respectful. Some villagers took pleasure in our suffering, for example, encouraging us to pull out the good seedlings instead of the weeds so they could witness the team leader scold us. Mingcheng, on the other hand, would always make sure he taught us thoroughly or let us do the easy tasks. We considered ourselves lucky if we were assigned to work in his group.

One day, before sending everyone out to level the field, our team leader asked Mingcheng to take a group out to bag the sesame. "Sesame is the main source of our pocket money so you must be careful to choose the right people to do this work," he reminded Mingcheng.

Sesame harvesting was delicate work. Every step, from cutting, binding and transporting the stalks to slowly drying them in the shade, to finally bagging the seeds, needed to be carried out with special care to prevent the tiny seeds from scattering. Once they fell to the ground, they could not be retrieved. Mingcheng chose me to be on his team. I was very pleased to work under his leadership and to be considered a "right person".

"Well, everyone can be a right person if they want to. I chose you because of my mother. She wants you to draw a picture for our tea table," Mingcheng told me.

His candid answer was disappointing but I didn't mind taking on the drawing job.

After work, I followed him home. His was not the usual home. In the front yard there was the normal corner toilet, pigsty and stacks of hay and stalks, but there were also flowerbeds bordered by shrubs and a large vegetable garden. These were covered by a tarpaulin now, but there was a dried dahlia wreath on his door and evergreen climbers on the window frame. His was a picket fence instead of the usual bare brick or timber. "In the summer, it'll be draped with climbers – vine tomatoes, peas, eggplants and cucumbers," he said proudly, and I was reminded of Fourth Grandma's little garden.

His house was simple but fresh and clean. A unique feature was an old bookcase, just like those that would be found in the city and, like those, empty except for a few of Chairman Mao's works.

Mingcheng's mother welcomed me. She was a smooth-skinned woman who wore finely cut garments and had a dignified smile. She showed me their tea table, a family heirloom. It was well-made and cleverly designed with four hidden drawers and four semi-circular drop leaves. The black surface gleamed from frequent polishing. She asked me to draw a picture on it.

What she wanted was not the usual pumpkins, cabbages or grasshoppers but a Beijing laneway with a traditional residential gate. She showed me a well-worn photo of such a gate with a young boy standing beside it.

"That's Mingcheng," she said. "He grew up in that courtyard in the South District of Beijing. He misses it. I want him to see that gate whenever he sits at this table for his meals." Seeing my surprise, she said, "I'll tell you the whole story, but let's have dinner first."

I spent three nights sketching and engraving and learnt more about Mingcheng – but not the "whole story". His mother did not live with him. "I've worked for a big household in Beijing for thirty-three years so that's where Mingcheng grew up and went to school. I come here at this time every year to make his winter clothes. In May, I'll be here again to clean his winter gear."

She didn't explain why her son had ended up living in this village and I was curious. Gradually I pieced the story together from what his mother said and what I gleaned from Mingcheng himself and other villagers. Mingcheng's mother's bad origins were revealed when the Cultural Revolution started. It might have been that she was a landlord's widow or a landlord's daughter – no one really knew. She should have been deported from Beijing but the owner of the "big household" – a very senior cadre – would not part with her fine domestic skills. So the Red Guards persecuted her son, who had just enrolled in university. He was imprisoned and tortured for four months before being deported in 1966 to the Village of Guests, which took him in. His mother's employer put up the money to build this house he lived in and with the help of the villagers he had been settled here for ten years. Whether because of his skill as a labourer, his kind nature, or sympathy for his unfortunate fate, Mingcheng seemed to be well regarded in the village. I never heard a word against him.

Neither Mingcheng nor his mother named the owner of the "big household", nor did they ever mention Mingcheng's father. There were rumours, of course, that Mingcheng was the illegitimate son of the owner of the "big household" and that he had been tortured because the Red Guards wanted to get him to confess to the scandal so they could bring the old man down. Mingcheng's loyalty to his father, the rumours went, had destroyed his future in the city.

Most villagers didn't believe this story even though they took delight in telling it. But I was sure this was not a rumour but the truth. I knew what unimaginable things had happened during the Cultural Revolution. I knew it from the saga of my own family.

Whenever I met a new friend among the villagers, I would consult with Immortal Zheng and his wife, my guardians. They just said, "Mingcheng and his mother have suffered a cruel fate, but they're trustworthy people."

After I finished the drawing for his mother, Mingcheng and I became friends. I found out that Mingcheng had read more widely than even most of my classmates had. So we talked a lot about the books we had both read. His intelligence also attracted other graduates, including Ying. Often, during a break, a group of us would engage him in conversation about literature, philosophy, the world situation and many other interesting things. However, we didn't talk about the Cultural Revolution.

In late January, Mingcheng did not come to work for a few days and there was some gossip about him buying a wife from a poor mountain village. As soon as he reappeared, Ying and I approached him, asking if this was true. When he confirmed it, Ying challenged him: "How can you, a well-educated man steeped in literature, end up buying a wife?"

I asked, "Is someone from Beijing forcing you into this?" hoping he would stave off our disappointment by saying yes.

Mingcheng smiled wryly, "Forced? Am I worth being forced by important people from Beijing? I'm nothing now and I need to get married." When he saw our stunned reaction, he quoted a classical saying, "'When one's heart is still and stops desiring, one is able to adapt to every circumstance.' My mother's only wish is to see me married and produce a grandchild for her. At my age and with my history, I can't be choosy."

"But we've talked about resilience, the meaning of life and so many things. I thought you meant what you said." It was my turn to challenge him.

"Yes, but they're just wonderful ideas. I'm not a city person anymore and I can't afford to have ideas now." He was beginning to sound frustrated.

I was silenced by his words, while Ying continued, "Chairman Mao says, 'If one is determined and scared of nothing, one will overcome all difficulties and –'" Mingcheng walked away before she had finished.

Later on, Ying expressed her great disappointment to our other roommates: "We regarded him as one of us but now he is behaving like a typical peasant!"

This time I didn't add my voice because Mingcheng's reference to the loss of his city identity reminded me of my own near-miss on this account. If Aunt Li hadn't burned my oldest brother Yang's letter and instead let the Red Guards deport my mother and me to a remote village, I could have turned into a Mingcheng and lived a life without choices.

I went to see Immortal Zheng about Mingcheng. He thought for a while, then said, "Mingcheng has decided to accept his fate. The more he has to do with you city lot, the harder his life will be. Just let him settle." His words made really clear to me that it was only because of my identity as a city graduate that I was able to live cheerfully in the village. It was this identity that prevented me from being oppressed by the backward rural practices and gave me hope of an eventual escape from the village.

More than six months later and after six rejections, Mingcheng was finally able in September 1977 to bring home a girl from the poorest and most remote village deep on Twenty Mile Long Mountain. He was so preoccupied by his marriage quest that we had hardly any chance to chat.

Unfortunately, the marriage turned out to be a disaster. To the girl from the poorest mountain village he was "an old bastard" and his mother was "a bad element". His new wife threw tantrums constantly. Mingcheng tolerated this at first but when his mother contracted cancer and came to live with them in the winter, the fights broke out. His wife refused to look after her sick mother-in-law and he started beating her. Domestic violence was common in Chinese villages, but when I learnt Mingcheng had become a wife-beater, I felt like crying. Ying and I tried to visit him but he refused to answer the door. He broke off contact with all the graduates. In the end, I adopted Zheng's advice, and "let him settle" into his fate.

During my second year in the village, I had asked Immortal Zheng to ask his brother, our team leader, to let me do all kinds of jobs. I wanted to experience village life to the full, in all its aspects. The team leader praised me publicly as an exemplar of Chairman Mao's youth, "fearing neither hardship nor death". The truth was that I had found the repetitive work in the fields boring, though physically it had become less demanding. So while the other female graduates worked day after day weeding, sowing and thinning seedlings, I was sent to build barns in the spring, to transport the wheat when it was harvested from the field to the threshing ground in the summer, to pack up the grain in the autumn and to look after the horses in the winter.

Horses were the treasure of the village and our second team owned three. During the harvest season, they were put hard to work, so in the winter they had to be given extra care. It was common knowledge that graduates were scared of big animals. When I asked the team leader to let me take care of the horses, he was so taken aback by this extraordinary request that he simply agreed. I was beside myself.

From a very young age, I had rescued injured birds, fed stray cats and talked to caged beasts at the zoo. I loved animals and felt an innate closeness with them. My mother had joked that in my previous incarnation I must have abused animals and was now having to repay my debt. When I was little this joke had made me even more dutiful towards animals. As I grew older, my mistrust of people strengthened my relationship with four-legged, winged and finned creatures. I was always delighted whenever there was a chance to be near them and to serve them.

I took the three horses to the commune vet to have them checked, walked them to a mountain village fifteen kilometres away to get them reshod by an expert farrier, and for a month slept in the warehouse where the stable was, to give them their extra night feed. They needed to be ready for the coming year's spring sowing and autumn harvest.

I loved that job.

In the month that I slept in the warehouse, I had to get up every night at midnight and again at three in the morning to feed mixed beans to the horses. Every time I walked into the stable, they all lifted their heads to greet me, their beautiful large eyes gazing at me thoughtfully. It gave me so much pleasure to watch them munch on the beans. I spent hours brushing them and talking to them.

The most valued of the horses, the shaft horse, was so notoriously bad-tempered that even our most experienced driver had to take great care when he put her in the shafts. It was said she had kicked a great many people, including a vet. That winter, she developed an infection on her neck, caused by a broken belt on the shaft rubbing against her neck. The pain made her temper worse. The vet injected her with antibiotics and gave us ten packets of anti-inflammatory powder. "Dissolve one packet in hot water and wash her neck with it and apply a hot compress every day for twenty minutes. If the infection can't be cleared up, the horse will have to be destroyed."

That evening, when I went to fill the water trough, I saw Jinlin, our team's driver, standing next to the shaft horse and crying. He was in his late thirties and known widely as a shy man. The villagers rarely heard him say anything except to give orders to the horses. People believed he must have had a speech problem, a bad stutter perhaps, but his wife and children swore he did not. He was very kind to animals and had a cat and a dog that he overindulged, according to the villagers. Because of this and his poor social skills, he had been permanently assigned to driving the horse-drawn cart and was considered the village's best driver.

To my surprise, Jinlin began to talk non-stop while he wiped away his tears. He feared the horse's days were numbered because no one would be able to apply the hot compress. He certainly was not game to do it. "You know she broke that vet's arm last year during her annual check-up. That's why he didn't want to treat her. If he can't do it, how can I?" He blamed himself for not having discovered the broken belt earlier, cursing both his cowardice and the horse's bad temper. He was very articulate. I felt an immediate empathy with him and his reserve with people and openness to animals. When we were with animals, we both felt safe.

When I said that I was prepared to give it a go, he thought I was mad. "I know you city people want to impress us so you can go back earlier, but don't do this. It's too dangerous."

"That's not why I want to do it," I insisted. "I love the horses and they love me too."

I was not exaggerating. I had given the horses nicknames, and they responded to my calls. I would take them to a field where carrots had been harvested, pick up the leftovers and put them in my overcoat pockets, then lie in the field under the sun, smelling the newly ploughed soil and call them one by one to take a carrot from my pocket. They would nudge my face and neck with their big muzzles to express their appreciation. If a horse I had not called came over, I would speak sternly to her and she would turn back, snort to apologise, or perhaps to complain. I felt I belonged with them and that we understood one another perfectly so I believed the shaft horse would allow me to help her.

Jinlin did not dare tell the team leader that I would be treating the horse. He knew what the response would be, because the team leader would not want to be responsible for any harm coming to a graduate. It was said that for days after he had given me the job of looking after the horses, the team leader had regretted it. The irony was that even though we were here to be re-educated, our city lives still seemed to be more valuable than those of the villagers – despite Mao's claims to the contrary.

The infection was on the left side of the horse's neck. Jinlin taught me to pull the horse's right rein tight to allow no distance between the horse's right cheek and the post. That way she would not be able to swing her head to the left to bite me. In the meantime, I had to stand right next to the horse's head so that when she kicked, I would be clear of her hind legs. "Watch her ears at all times. If she flattens them, be really careful."

The skin on the left side of her neck was swollen and broken. When I approached her with the steaming hot cloth soaked in medicine, her eyes were opened wide, huge and full of fear. How vulnerable she must have felt. At that moment, my sympathy and sense of responsibility overpowered my own fear. Her ears were completely flattened and she bucked and kicked madly, but I did not stop. I kept applying the hot compress to her wound while I talked to her softly. She gradually stopped kicking and began to prick up her ears. In the end she was even snorting; the medicine must have soothed her pain.

Every time I approached her to give her the treatment, the horse was tense at first but then relaxed. Each time she relaxed a little more quickly and on the last two days she greeted me and my bucket with snorting and pawing, merely a gentle warning. Meanwhile, the swelling on her neck was significantly reduced.

I applied the treatment at night so that our team leader wouldn't see me and try to stop me. I didn't want the horse to die! But when I was down to the last packet of medicine, I decided to show off what I had done. I washed the horse in the morning and left her untied. Jinlin and the team leader were amazed to see I could treat the horse without binding her to the post.

The infection was gone and the horse and I had formed a close bond. When we went to the vet for a check-up, I rode her without a saddle each way, further shocking my team leader. This episode produced two good outcomes: I became a confidante of Jinlin, and the only female driver in the whole commune. I valued the friendship with Jinlin and took great pride in my new job.

When we worked together from then on, Jinlin talked a lot, always about animals. When a cat caught a mouse, he told me, we mustn't disturb it so that the cat could enjoy its feast; we should never say hurtful things to a dog because dogs understood everything; and whipping horses for no reason was heartless. "The drivers will be cursed because heaven has eyes," he said. It was he who had insisted that I be given the top job of alternative driver during the next wheat harvest and would not hear a "no" from the team leader.

Transporting the wheat after it was harvested was a special job. Each horse-drawn cart needed to be loaded, in my team leader's words, "as high as the headquarters building", the tallest in the village. Two separate skills were required of the two-person team: the driver on the ground had to pick up the wheat bales with a three-metre-long fork, fashioned from a very light tree branch, and load them onto the cart at the exact spot indicated by the person on the cart. This was a demanding job as it was difficult to manoeuvre the heavy wheat bale with such a long-handled fork. The alternate driver on the cart had to build hundreds of these bales into a huge inverted trapezoid, two or three times as wide on top as the base of the cart and perfectly balanced. If either of the drivers did a bad job, the load would tip and the whole thing collapse.

I mastered my "top" skills on the first day. When the cart was fully laden and we headed back to the village, I perched on top, balancing the load, the treetops brushing against me, feeling I could almost touch the sky. It was bliss.

Jinlin and I became working partners from the wheat harvest to the autumn harvest. In the autumn of 1977, he let me drive our cart, one of the Village of Guests' three carts, to deliver our production team's grain quota to the government. He helped me trim the manes and tails of our three horses and put red tassels on their foreheads. When I drove my cart through the gate of the delivery compound, everyone cheered.

So I became famous in the region. Wherever I went, people pointed and said, "She's that female graduate driver."

Deeply immersed as I became in village life, my view of the villagers changed. I was awed by their generosity, honesty and kindness. Their rude manners remained, but I no longer regarded them with urban contempt. I wanted instead to introduce them to some of the delicacies I had enjoyed in the city. Every time I had a break in Beijing, I would buy cakes, candies, snacks and even chocolates for my village friends. I could never get enough for them and wished that I had more pocket money and fewer friends.

In contrast, I was almost an outsider in my own group. Except for my roommates, I rarely associated with the other graduates. Much had happened among them during the eighteen months. Many of the girls, for example, had been overwhelmed by the hard labour, by homesickness and by despair about the future, while I was enjoying my various jobs. They would gather in the canteen, lamenting their lot and reinforcing one another's misery. Some formed liaisons with other graduates, and one or two even got pregnant, which led to public naming, shaming and abortions.

Some of the boys were becoming restless and started making trouble by stalking, teasing or bullying some of the girls.

One day, when I went to the canteen to have lunch with Ying and my other roommates, a boy from our second team called out to me, "Hi, someone would like to ask you a question."

I stood there, holding a bowl of rice soup and a steamed bun, and watched him giggling madly with a crowd of boys standing around. Something didn't look right.

"Who? What question?"

"Come on!"

"Go, go, go!"

"Don't be scared by a girl. Tell her the truth!"

Another boy stood up; he was also from our team and had worked as my loader for a few days when I was the alternate driver. He walked over to me and said, "If you think I've taken a fancy to you, you'd better think again. You should try to write a better love letter for a start."

I was totally dumbfounded. "What do you mean?"

The boy blushed and looked around for someone to help him out while the onlookers were doubled over with laughter.

I knew I was being teased though I had no idea about what. "How dare you?" I screamed, and hurled the soup bowl and the bun at him. In the dead silence that followed, I stormed out of the canteen.

When Ying came back to our room, I was sitting on the *kang*, crying. "I didn't write him a letter. He's a liar," I blurted out.

"Of course you didn't. Everyone knows that."

"What do you mean?" I asked, even more confused.

"He just wanted to get your attention. He likes you but you've ignored him. Can't you see he was being urged on by the others? They all do these things to get the girls going. You've been too harsh."

"Did they do this to you too?"

"Unfortunately no one likes me."

Ying's candid reply surprised me. Before I could ask any further questions, she resumed her role as group leader. "Look, what they did to you was wrong. In fact, the morale of our whole group is not good right now. I will talk to the other leaders to see what we can do. But you have to admit that you've been disconnected from everyone else. Did you see how you hurt him? Fortunately the soup was not hot, otherwise it would have burnt his face."

I didn't regret what I had done. I had no interest in dating and I hated mob culture. All I wanted was to be part of village life – since I had to live here, I must, as my mother had once advised Immortal Zheng, "accept reality" and remember that "an empty life was not worth living". I was single-minded about this and I didn't care what the other graduates thought about me.

Ying and the other youth leaders didn't manage to raise morale, and the disturbances among the boys grew day by day. Some of them started drinking heavily and going to other villages to pick fights. In early October of 1977, a group of our male graduates had a bloody fight with the graduates at a neighbouring commune. Fourteen boys were seriously injured and hospitalised, five of them ours.

This incident was reported in the *Regional News Daily*. At a specially summoned village meeting, Jia spoke on behalf of the commune leaders, giving us all a dressing-down and ordering each production team leader to assign us to the hardest jobs.

"They're restless from overeating! Tire them out with back-breaking toil!" he shouted during the meeting.

But most of the villagers just felt sorry for the injured boys. They boiled eggs or killed chickens to prepare special food for the patients. When some boys cried, they comforted them: "Take it easy. The pain will be gone soon. Ignore Jia's nonsense. He's not human. All those meetings in the town damaged his brain."

The villagers' words quickly spread among the graduates and surprised everyone. This was certainly a different slant on political propaganda! Moreover, saying someone was not human, that they were heartless and lacked human feelings, was the severest judgment the village could bring down. All of us, and me in particular, felt justified. We were so used to being placed in "the other register" that it was a revelation to hear that, for the villagers, that was where Jia belonged, not us. I was even more pleased about my immersion in the Village of the Guests.

12
The Exam

After our second autumn break in early October 1977, one of the older graduates, a girl with high-ranking military parents, failed to return to the village. The rules regarding holiday breaks were strict. We were not allowed to return to Beijing outside of the three legitimate breaks and a late return to the village meant punishment: hard labour, public denunciation and a bad mark on your record. No one had dared break the rules, so this incident caused a disturbance among the graduates and annoyed some of the village leaders.

The director of the village's birth control committee, Ms Li, had only recently become involved with the graduates after a couple of the girls became pregnant. She came to investigate and asked the girl's boyfriend if he had made his girlfriend pregnant. The boy stoutly denied it. Nor did he have any idea why she hadn't come back.

A week later, a truck sent by the girl's family arrived at the village. The driver left a letter for her boyfriend and took her things away. Howling desperately, the boyfriend ran from his dormitory with her letter in his hand. "She's been reassigned to Beijing, to work in 301 Military Hospital! She did not bother to tell me or even say goodbye!"

I joined everyone outside the dormitory hoping to find out more. I felt sorry for the boy, but my focus, like everyone else's, was on what this news implied.

In theory, all graduates would eventually be reassigned back to Beijing but no one in the government had ever brought this up in the last two years. The older graduates had been here for nearly four years and they were restless. While this news was devastating for the girl's boyfriend, it was exciting for everyone else because no matter how much power the girl's father wielded, he would not have been able to achieve this outcome if reassignment had not already been on the agenda.

In the evening, I went with the other graduates to brigade headquarters and demanded to be told the truth. The number-one person in our village was the party secretary, Mr Zhang, an agreeable elder. He did not normally deal with us but that evening he did talk to us. Apparently, reassignment was supposed to have started after the harvest, but for some reason it had been put on hold. He promised that as soon as he received any news, he would let us know.

We all felt uneasy. During the September break, I had heard plenty of rumours through Dong and my father. The nation remained unsettled after Chairman Mao's death in September 1976. There had been a power struggle at the top. An extreme left clique, later known as the Gang of Four and led by Mao's widow, Jiang Qing, wanted to press on with the harsh policies of the Cultural Revolution, while a moderate camp under Deng Xiaoping was determined to end the turbulence. Nearly one year on, the nation was still in a state of uncertainty and apprehension, even though the moderate camp had triumphed and the Gang of Four had been arrested and officially blamed for the decade-long chaos of the Cultural Revolution.

"That's probably why there's been no change in your village," Dong said in response to my question about why Jia still held absolute power over us and bullied us at will, even though the Cultural Revolution had ended.

Now, after hearing what Mr Zhang had said, I was sure that we had been forgotten. I remembered Chairman Mao's repeated exhortation, "There is no revolution without sacrifice." The thought that I was doomed to spend the rest of my life in the village came back to haunt me.

A couple of weeks later, Dong wrote to tell me that the twenty million city graduates in every part of China shared my concern that the change in the leadership might jeopardise our reassignment. There had been petitions and demonstrations everywhere. The government asked the graduates to be patient because change needed time.

His letter further depressed me. I became sceptical about the new political regime. How long could it last? We had heard so often that the great Communist Party could correct its wrongs; I wondered whether there would be enough time for the changes to be implemented before this present correction would itself be found to be wrong.

I was like a person recovered from amnesia. My mind was suddenly very clear: I was not one of the village's own and mine should be a different future. *Yes, I have lived a wonderful life in the Village of Guests, but that is precisely because I have been just a guest.* Mingcheng had summed up his fate well: "I'm not a city person anymore. I can't afford to have wonderful ideas." If I ended up losing my city graduate identity, my dream of living a life like my mother's, of travelling the world, would also become an idea I couldn't afford to have.

Preoccupied by these thoughts, I became subdued. Jinlin observed this change in my demeanour and said to me, "Xiyan, you can't be absent-minded when you're dealing with large animals. I know you graduates have all become restless lately. Go and talk to the team leader, it would be better if you worked with your group for a while."

I nodded absent-mindedly. He let out a deep sigh.

One week later, there was an accident while I was collecting manure. During my tea break in a villager's house, some kids teased one of my leading horses. Normally I would have picked up the signs – she was pawing the ground and the whites of her eyes were showing – but I was preoccupied and failed to do the usual checks. As soon as I released the brake and waved the whip to start the cart, she shied and took off at a gallop. Although she couldn't go too fast because we were going uphill, the track was rough and the cart was jolting wildly. I ran beside the cart and applied the brake firmly but it had no impact at all. The cart hit a large pothole and overturned.

I fell over but managed to jump straight back up. The horse that had originally bolted had stopped but my shaft horse was pinned flat on her back. I knew she was pregnant and I was frightened for her. If something happened to her, the village would lose two horses. I tried to free her from the harness but I couldn't remove the heavy timber shaft from her neck. People came running from everywhere. "Are you all right?" they shouted.

"I'm fine. Please," I yelled back, "help me lift this to free her!"

As soon as the shaft was removed, the horse stood up, shook herself violently to get rid of the dust and neighed loudly. I checked her and she seemed to be okay. In the meantime, the villagers had already righted the cart and were shovelling the manure back onto it.

"Go home," one man told me. "We've sent someone to call Driver Jinlin. You go and have a break. Thank heaven nobody's hurt."

I felt guilty, even though everybody was encouraging me to go home, and insisted on helping with the reloading, but when I went to pick up a shovelful of manure, I realised I couldn't use my left arm. I dropped the shovel and went back to my dormitory without saying anything to anyone. When I took off my thick jacket and saw the bone sticking out above my elbow, the pain suddenly hit me and I lost it. I sat down on the floor, crying and screaming, until a crowd of villagers rushed in. Later I learnt that I kept on saying, "I'm going to die here. I don't want to die here."

It took an hour for them to get me to the regional hospital by tractor, along a bumpy country road, and it was dark by the time we got there. Unfortunately, the hospital's electricity had been cut that evening so the X-ray and any operation had to be postponed till the morning. I waited all night on a stretcher in a dark room and in the process developed a fever.

Although they set the bone the next day, I was in a bad way, feverish and tearful. Even Jia was worried so he granted me a week's paid leave to return to Beijing to recover. His decision only intensified my misery because I remembered that I no longer had a home of my own, and I didn't want to go to my father's. In the end, I had my one-week break in the village. My team leader delivered two dozen eggs and three chickens from the village farm to Immortal Zheng's house and asked his wife to prepare a week's worth of a convalescent diet for me.

I had been regarded as tough, so my breakdown surprised the villagers. I was surprised by my reaction to the accident, too, because I had never lost control like that before. However, before I had a chance to think all of this through, news of the resumption of the University Entrance Examinations arrived at the village. It was 21 October 1977.

This was a clear reversal of Mao's policy. Although some university departments had reopened in the early 1970s, there had been no entrance exams. Admission was by family origin, so those who were admitted as students were the children of peasants, workers and soldiers. The reintroduction of the entrance exams confirmed that the Cultural Revolution had well and truly ended and the changes were real. Secretary Zhang kept his promise and broke the news to us as soon as he had finished his "important meeting" in the commune. The examinations would be for high school graduates from the last eleven years, and would take place in early December for an intake the following March. With this in the offing, many other things had to be put on hold, including the reassignment of the city graduates.

This news was like a rope to a drowning person for me. I was the first of the fourteen graduates who put their names on the candidate list. But when the official registration forms arrived, many balked. Some did not bother completing their registration when they saw that the forms still asked about family origins, which led them to believe that the academic merit-based entrance examination was yet another empty promise; others were intimidated by questions such as "preference of study major" because we had become so accustomed to submitting to the party's orders and had lost the ability to make decisions for ourselves. In addition, after ten years without access to tertiary education, hardly anyone in my age group understood the options.

My heart did indeed sink at the question about family origins. If this was a criterion, I would be the first to be excluded, no matter how brilliant my academic results. I came to this conclusion because of the special treatment I had received after Chairman Mao's death, even though I had tried hard to forget that episode.

When the news of Chairman Mao's death reached the countryside on 10 September 1976, I had been on my way to Yang's Town as Driver Jinlin's assistant. We had been sent to the commune there to buy ready-cut sandstone blocks. This was an exciting job, travelling along a country road, lunching out and earning an extra 25 fen as a travel allowance. We loaded the blocks then stopped at an inn that, according to Jinlin, was famous for its meat pancakes. We watched enthralled as the chef mixed the fillings, rolled out the dough and slid the enormous pancakes onto a giant wok. Suddenly, the PA system crackled into life and the breaking news was broadcast. Everybody was ordered to drop whatever they were doing and assemble at village headquarters. Jinlin and I wrapped up our pancakes and rushed back to our village.

Headquarters at our village was already draped in mourning with white flowers and curtains and the villagers were lined up in front of a huge portrait of Chairman Mao, waiting to farewell "the greatest leader". Jia was giving a speech emphasising that during the funeral period people had to be vigilant against the "bad elements" in the village to prevent any possible upheaval. These bad elements were seven former landlords and rich farmers we had been introduced to the day we had arrived. However, as soon as our team leader spotted me, he walked over and started to lead me away.

"Where are you taking me? I haven't paid my respects to Chairman Mao."

He didn't utter a word until we got out of the crowd. "Sorry, Xiyan, Jia wants you locked up too." He turned away to avoid looking at me. "Look, it's nothing personal. He said that you're the only one who meets the lock-up criteria – 'bad origins' compounded by having an 'active reactionary' on your family record. You know Chairman Mao's death is too serious a matter and everyone has to obey orders from above."

I did exactly what I had done when I was excluded from welcoming the foreign leaders in high school. I said I would fully comply with the authority's decision, but I was frightened. I didn't know what being locked up would mean for me.

I was escorted to a storeroom, the temporary prison, where I met my fellow "bad elements", the seven former landlords and rich farmers. We were locked up for hours while the memorial ceremony went on. The seven played cards. "We're used to this," they said to me, "but you're still a bit young for it. Look, don't worry, this is just for show."

Their kind words calmed me down. Thinking over the various humiliations in my past assured me this one would also soon be over. I watched them play and tried to forget what was really happening. As soon as we were released from the storeroom, I went back to my horse and cart as if nothing had happened. That evening, Immortal Zheng invited me to his house for dinner. He and his wife didn't mention the incident, but they loaded the table with scrumptious dishes to cheer me up. I never gave anyone a chance to mention the incident and buried it deep in my memory until I was faced with the exam registration form.

Listen, you, I said to myself over and over during yet another sleepless night, *you cannot fold your hands and wait for destruction!* I repeated my mother's advice: *You must put up a fight even when things seem hopeless.*

In the end there were just five names on the list of university admittance registrations. There was Chen, a tall man from the first production team who had been in the village for four years. He was regarded as the most intelligent of the graduates and had therefore been assigned to teach in the village primary school. There were Lan and Hui, shy twin sisters from a military cadre's family who kept to themselves, from the third production team; and then there were Ying and myself, from the second production team.

I took a form for Bing and persuaded him to register as well.

"This could be your only chance to satisfy your passion for books," I said to him.

He was hesitant. "What if I can't pass the exams?"

"You'll never know if you don't try," I said.

I went to see his father and promised that Bing and I would prepare for the exam together. His father agreed in the hope that this might rescue Bing from marrying the girl with vitiligo.

In choosing universities or majors, I was clear about two things: I wanted to study literature, and I had to find a university that would pay my living expenses. So I chose my major as literature and put down three universities – Beijing Normal University, Beijing Teachers' College and Beijing Broadcasting College. The first two offered a free dormitory as well as an 18-yuan monthly stipend.

The production brigade leaders gave all of us candidates a break to prepare for the exams, which were in five weeks' time. Four of them went back to Beijing, but I stayed on, since I had promised Bing we would study together.

After my injury, I had been given the most important job in a village, that of labour recorder. This involved writing down each morning the work assignment of each person in our team and then walking to every post twice a day to call the roll. Each villager's annual remuneration – how many kilos of grain a person would get for the following year and how much cash they would be awarded after deducting their grain provision – was calculated by the brigade accountant at the end of the year based solely on the labour recorder's workbook. It was not unusual to hear of village recorders being attacked for mistakes.

The previous recorder had been assaulted by someone who accused him of inflating his own family's working days. This had happened at the time of my accident and my team leader saw me as the perfect replacement. I was a graduate, I was capable and I got on well with everyone on the team. Most importantly, I was an outsider. I could not be suspected of corrupt behaviour on behalf of a relative. Even though I was close to Immortal Zheng, no one believed that the Zheng family would need or seek my help.

This job meant I was on my own most of the time and the long walks between the fields became excellent opportunities for reciting the facts of literature, history, geography and mathematical formulae that two years in the village had leached from my brain. There was so much knowledge that I needed to recommit to memory.

Most of the old textbooks had been destroyed during the Cultural Revolution on the grounds that they served the old "poisonous" education system. After the news broke of the resumption of the university entrance examinations, the whole nation rushed to rediscover these works. Some revised versions were quickly printed. Seven million, three hundred thousand copies of *Teach Yourself Mathematics, Physics and Chemistry* were printed, but this was still not enough to meet the demand. People rummaged through recycling stations in the hope of finding old dumped books. I was lucky with my study materials, however. Because of my friendship with Bing, I had been gathering textbooks and learning materials for over a year. He was particularly good in mathematics so I had even found a book from 1964 called *Mathematics Revision Materials for the University Entrance Examination*. This material had now become a treasure trove.

I managed my time carefully to ensure that I would have reviewed everything by the time the examination came around. Every night, I covered a new section of each subject and copied the key information into a small book. I took the small book with me as I carried out my labour-recording duties and memorised those key points. After work, I recounted to Bing what I had memorised. This saved Bing a lot of reading time while it consolidated my understanding as I talked through what I had learnt.

All was going to plan until three weeks later when I received a letter from my father. He had learnt from Dong – who was also a candidate – that I had registered and chosen to study literature. He was furious that I had not consulted him. He recounted all his ups and downs since 1957 as evidence that science had always brought him glory while literature had led to nothing but trouble. He told me that I must switch from literature to science. "If there comes a day when you study literature at university, I'll die with my eyes open."

Dying with one's eyes open meant dying with eternal regrets. Only the most unloving child would cause this kind of grief to a parent. I was horrified and begged Immortal Zheng's son to ask the commune leader if my form could be changed. Too late, I was told, unless I wanted to withdraw my candidature. I was at a crossroads. When I talked it over with Immortal Zheng, he asked me, "What would your mother say?"

I looked at the happy face of my mother in their group photo and remembered her last words. "She would like me to have a life."

"So stop crying and get on with your preparations. Who knows, you might not even pass so your father won't have to worry at all. But in the end, at least you'll have been a candidate."

Immortal Zheng had never spoken to me so firmly. I could even sense a trace of anger towards my father, who was wielding his authority over me for his own purposes, and perhaps also with me, for wanting to give up. He had never talked about my parents' marriage, but at that moment I had no doubt that he knew of my mother's frustration. I felt he was standing in for my mother who would be urging me to make my *own* decisions.

I wiped my eyes and said, "Thank you. I will get on with my preparation." I didn't reply to my father's letter.

The days of the exam, 9 and 10 December for our region, finally arrived. All candidates sat for the Chinese literature, mathematics, and politics exams. The science candidates sat for a combined physics and chemistry paper while the literary arts candidates had history and geography. Each exam was three hours long.

Our exams were held in the commune's high school. Secretary Zhang ordered a small tractor to take the five of us and Bing to town. We were amazed to see the high school surrounded by at least forty fully armed policemen. Of the approximately eighty candidates, only a handful were local youngsters.

There were hundreds of onlookers come to see why anyone would bother to suffer like this. Inside, names and photos were stuck on desks. Holding our exam permission card, which had our photo on it, each of us was led to the desk that had our name on it and, after a careful double check, we were allowed to sit down. The twins Lan and Hui caused no end of trouble because no one could tell them apart. The supervisors were too nervous to decide which twin was the right one to sit at which desk so the police chief was called in. After a few minutes' debate, he ordered them to sit far apart in order to make sure they didn't play any tricks.

It took almost an hour to seat everyone, and the atmosphere was extremely tense. I was worried that all this might be too overwhelming for Bing. I had noticed when he came in that his face flushed scarlet.

The bell rang and folded exam papers were placed on each desk. We were told to start. When everyone opened their papers, there was a unanimous gasp – it was 1.2 metres long! A loud thud came from the back of the room – a female candidate had fainted. In the chaos, I turned to look at Bing; his face was drenched in sweat.

I completed the first paper, language and literature, and felt satisfied with my answers. The first section tested common literary knowledge, such as who was the first Chinese poet and who wrote *War and Peace*. This was followed by essays in classical Chinese to be translated into modern Chinese. The third section was literary analysis and the concluding part was a composition titled "Myself in This Year of Combat". I answered all the questions and wrote a one-page essay.

Unfortunately, the composition task sealed Bing's fate. He was confused by the words "year of combat". As a country boy, he was not familiar with this kind of political metaphor. A good essay should have smoothly linked what the candidate had said and done during the year with the victory of Deng Xiaoping's camp over the Gang of Four.

"What could I write?" Bing said as we walked out. "I didn't know there *was* a war this year."

I bit my tongue but Ying explained the metaphor to him. He said nothing but looked defeated. The next morning he fainted at his desk and was sent back home.

I was so focused during the exam that I didn't know until the lunch break that Bing had left. I felt really bad when I learnt he would not be returning for the last exam. I thought we had covered everything he would need to know, but I had overlooked two things: growing up in a village and educated in easy-going country schools, Bing had not been exposed to much of the assumed knowledge that we city graduates took for granted, and he also lacked the experience of handling high-stakes exams. Chen told us that exams were a joke in the village primary school, often involving copying out textbooks, and it was not much better in the commune's high school. No wonder Bing broke down under extreme pressure. I worried that he would be subjected to even more bullying by the villagers and began to see my passionate encouragement of him as irresponsible. But while I was concerned about Bing, I couldn't give him too much attention right then because I had more exams to deal with.

After the mathematics and geography exams, I felt even more confident. I remembered every single question and knew from discussing them with other candidates afterwards that I had achieved 98 per cent for both papers. I was so exhausted when I finally walked out of the exam room that even the setting winter sun dazzled me. But I was happy; I had the sense of a mission successfully accomplished.

The five of us were waiting outside the commune department store for our tractor to pick us up when the commune leader walked up to us. When he heard my name, he said, "Oh, you're the one who wanted to change your choice. Tell your father not to worry – even if you pass the exams, there's still the medical check and political investigation. Still a long way to go."

He was trying to be helpful, but all his comforting words did was alarm me.

13

The Verdict

After a five-week wait, the village received a call from the commune on 16 January. Four candidates had passed the first round and would have their medical check and political investigation the following week. The two who had failed were Bing and Lan. Sad as we were for the others, Chen, Ying, Hui and I were beside ourselves with excitement, even though we knew that only half of the successful first rounders would go through to the next stage.

The medical check took place in the hospital in the neighbouring commune of Yang's Town two days later. The four of us borrowed bicycles from our village friends and cycled twenty kilometres to get there. We were so worried that the doctors might find some defect that even Ying kept saying, "I hope my missing tooth won't be a problem."

Fortunately, all four of us survived the check without a hitch. Straight afterwards, Ying and Hui left for Beijing for their Chinese New Year holiday. They had one thing in common, good family origins, so they were not at all concerned about the following day's political investigation. On the other hand, Chen, the son of a former factory owner, and I both had politically blemished fathers, so we stayed in the village, hoping that thus exhibiting our humility would help us do better in the political investigation.

My dormitory was directly behind and backed onto brigade headquarters. From my back fence I saw the village leaders begin to gather there after dinner on 19 January: the three production team leaders; Mr Jia, the director of the village city graduates who had received us so harshly on our arrival and locked me up when Mao died; Ms Li, the director of the birth control committee; and Mr Zhang, the party secretary. They had all changed into their good clothes and wore serious expressions. So, this was a big event for the village as well as for me. I desperately wanted to know how they were going to go about deciding my fate.

Most of the graduates had left for the New Year's break, which had been extended to six weeks because everybody was so unsettled. I was the only one left in my dorm. After our first harvest, we had had stoves installed to heat our bedrooms in the winter. The stove in my room was dead just then, which gave me an idea. I pretended to have no knowledge of what was going on at headquarters, and went to ask Limper Lieu for a half-burned briquette.

There were two rooms in headquarters. The big one was the official meeting venue, while the small one functioned as the broadcast studio, Limper Lieu's office, and his sleeping quarters. One of his jobs was to make tea for guests so his stove was always burning nicely and his kettle was always full and on the boil. His office was also next to the village co-op where graduates could buy stamps, toothpaste, biscuits and candies.

Many of us had become close to Limper Lieu. After work, there would always be two or three graduates sitting on his bed chatting with him as they soaked up the warmth, sometimes with a hot cup of tea. Whenever our stove died, we would get a half-burned briquette from him to revive it. Gradually we realised that he had gotten this job not only because of his crippled legs, but also for his sharp mind and smooth manner. During our entire stay in the village, none of us ever saw him lose his cool, no matter how difficult the situation.

Limper Lieu gave me a briquette and shooed me away – "You'd better keep your stove alive. I won't let you come in tonight and you know very well why."

Before I left, I glanced into the meeting room through the small glass pane Limper Lieu had installed so he could see who was coming into his office. To my great disappointment, all the participants were sitting in a circle playing poker.

I revived the stove and it warmed the dormitory, but I remained restless. A bold idea was brewing in my mind. The village's only public toilet was in the front yard of the headquarters building, between the meeting room and the co-op. We graduates often used it because it was also the only toilet not adjacent to a pigsty. I thought, *I could pretend to go to the toilet and eavesdrop on the meeting while I'm there.*

It was after eight o'clock when I walked out into the pitch-black night. In winter time, the villagers turned their lights off soon after dinner. I managed to follow my familiar mud path to the stable to see my horses. I was in the habit of sharing my insights with them so I asked them if I should eavesdrop and they seemed to nod. I knew eavesdropping was not a nice thing to do, yet ten minutes later there I was, squatting under the meeting room window. I was so desperate to know my fate that I didn't feel the cold or think about being caught.

"Hearts! Is Hui okay in your opinion?" Director Jia asked.

The third team leader responded. "Well – she's fine. Not too good a labourer though. Too finicky. Then again, it may not be Hui. One of the twins is good, so the finicky one may be her sister Lan –"

"So that's fine. Tick!" Secretary Zhang.

They started talking about me. My team leader Baolin went first: "She's the best we've ever had. Whatever you ask her to do, she does it well. She's probably the only one who can survive here."

No! I do not want to survive here. I wished I had not worked so hard.

Baolin went on to recount how I had saved the valuable shaft horse and how I showed respect to the locals. "Even the mute driver opens up to her. She's a benevolent girl and I definitely think she should be recommended. By the way, who's got the Queen of Hearts?"

"What about her father? Isn't he a Rightist or a reactionary?" Ms Li was disliked by all the graduates for her superiority and nosiness; the feeling was mutual.

"Indeed. She's not that clean herself either. Remember her father's letter? Three Jacks!" Director Jia again. "I know you like her because she's close to your brother but we are discussing a serious matter. We need to be very careful about recommending her and Chen."

I crouched in the dark, shivering.

"King!" shouted Secretary Zhang. "Listen, before we make our decision I'd like to say something. As you know, many graduates attended the exam. In our small area, there were six from the machinery factory, four from the Village of Gu, eleven from the Village of West and five from us. Guess what? Only six passed the first round and four of them were ours. What does this say? It says that we have re-educated them extremely well, particularly the two with family problems! They're the pride of our village so I put up both hands to recommend all of them. Ha, I win, the pot is mine."

The party secretary was the ultimate authority. Immediately I heard everyone agreeing with him.

"You're so damn right!"

"We definitely did a good job."

"Totally agree. But it's not fair you've won again."

I felt my heart would burst and I wanted to yell and jump for joy. Instead, I beat a hasty retreat and turned into the side lane to return to my dormitory. I was startled by a shadow springing out from side wall of the headquarters building, and quickly sprinting away. Chen! Great minds did think alike. I burst out laughing, quickly covering my mouth and hoping no one had heard me.

I left for Beijing the next day and ran into Chen at the bus stop. He snuck a look around and whispered, "Someone told me that our secretary decided to recommend all of us because we are the pride of the village."

"Who told you that? You're sure they're reliable?" I asked, playing dumb.

"Oh well, believe it or not – up to you. I don't betray people."

At the beginning of February 1978, on Chinese New Year's Eve, *The Beijing Daily* announced that university admission notices would be delivered to the successful candidates on 14 February. Everybody was buzzing with excitement.

Nine people in our Beijing residential compound had sat for the exam and three had got through the first round – me, a boy from the outer yard, and my brother Dong. They discovered during his medical check that Dong had hepatitis A and this cancelled his candidacy. He was devastated and didn't want to hear anything about the exam. My father was still angry because I had not changed my major, so at home we avoided the topic, which suited me because I didn't want to get my hopes up.

In fact, I spent very little time at home during this long break. Dong was seriously dating a pretty woman who two years later would become my sister-in-law. She was at our home every evening and he only had eyes for her. My father had been put in charge of the restoration of ancient buildings in Beijing. His office was at the gate of Jingshan Park, which was at the end of our street, so he was often home during the day.

Fortunately, by this time the ban on books and movies had been relaxed and the military compound was showing old movies every night. With my former classmate's help, I could get into the compound as a privileged guest. During the day, I would tell stories – mostly the plot of the movie I had seen the previous night – to my neighbours. Aunt Li was still our yard leader but she did not have to deal with "class struggles" anymore so she made her home available for my storytelling. Third Daughter was not among my audience for she too was busy dating a "nice man", according to Aunt Li.

On 13 February, a week before the end of our New Year break, Chen, Ying, Hui and I went back to the village. Our admissions notices would be delivered to the commune the next day if we had been successful. It was awkward because everyone knew why we were back early and that we might not be successful, but there was no other way to discover our fate. Hui did not dare sleep in her deserted dormitory and joined Ying and me in our village house. No one was in a mood to chat, so we turned in very early.

Surprisingly, I slept soundly and had a pleasant dream. My mother and I were sitting in the living room of Uncle Yuji's home. My uncle said to my mother: "Now little Bright Swallow seems fully fledged and you can relax."

He smiled at me and asked me to play piano for him. How could I? I had never learnt. I looked to my mother for help, but she simply said: "Just do it and you'll be fine."

And so it was – it was as if someone else was controlling my fingers and I could not stop. Then I heard the cock crow and woke up. It was 5:00 in the morning and still dark. What did the dream mean? My mother rarely appeared in my dreams. Was this an omen? Had I really passed?

Uncle Yuji was the most successful of my mother's siblings. A graduate in medicine, he had established his own hospital. He was a thoracic specialist whose patients included senior government cadres, including Deng Yingchao, the wife of the late Premier Zhou Enlai. His family lived a comfortable life in their own *siheyuan* (quadrangle). Their home represented the *other* culture, which my mother was comfortable in. In his living room were those rarities, a big TV, a piano and a set of sofas; in his courtyard, among the landscaped trees and flowers, were three large blue and white porcelain pots full of goldfish.

When I was little, my mother often took me to his home, where she appeared unusually relaxed, talking to her brother with a cup of coffee in her hand. She was like a fish that had been put back into the water. I once asked what they could have had to talk about. My mother replied: "All the books we've read, the knowledge we've acquired, and the things we've enjoyed in life. There are lots of beautiful things to discuss." A few weeks before her death, she took me with her for a last visit to her brother. He cooked stir-fried rice, tiny dumplings and my mother's favourite radish salad, hoping to whet her faded appetite. Not a word had been spoken.

Now I cried. I was sure the dream I had had was a message from my mother. But what if I failed her? I switched on the light and did something very unusual. I recorded my dream and my thoughts in my diary. I finished with a quote from Fourth Grandma: "Everything is predestined."

I had learnt very early that keeping diaries was dangerous. I had seen my mother throw her old diaries into the stove even before the Cultural Revolution, and I had attended public denunciation meetings where diaries were used as evidence. Diaries were supposedly personal, but in Mao's era nothing personal was respected. Ironically, diaries were the most popular gifts – apart from Mao's works – for birthdays, graduations, farewells and weddings. I had taken one with me to the village but most of the pages were still blank. However, that anxious morning I decided to take the risk. My mother's message was too significant to be forgotten.

It was still dark outside when I slipped the diary under the bamboo mat on the *kang*. I switched off the light and lay in the dark while my mind went off into flights of fancy. Had my mother had a role in rousing me from my complacency in the village? Had she somehow incited my "out of character" behaviour after my accident?

When the cock crowed the third time, I rose quietly. I decided to go to work, otherwise I would go mad waiting. Ying and Hui heard me and emerged from the other bedroom. They had had the same idea. After a quick bowl of porridge, we heard the bells and went to the gathering points – Hui to the third team's and Ying and me to the second's.

We were among the first to arrive. While we waited, we slipped our hands into our sleeves and swayed from foot to foot to warm ourselves in the winter-morning cold. Ying suddenly laughed. "Remember? When we first saw the peasants doing this, we thought they were so funny. Now, two years later, we're doing the same thing," she said, exaggerating her sway.

As I laughed, I thought, *In two more years we might be copying the village women and peeling off our clothes in public to catch lice.*

All three teams were sent to the end of the village to level out the common field, so Chen and Hui were there as well. The work was not demanding and the peasants were teasing one another. When different teams worked together, there were more chances to tease or flirt. The villagers were very conservative and if a young person had an affair or even showed interest in someone, their reputations would be trashed. On the other hand, their daily banter was all about sex. It didn't matter whether they were married or single, their talk was bawdy. They would even grab each other's genitals, as long as it was in public. After two years there, we had become used to this and sometimes joined in.

After lunch, all we could think of was the PA system. When would they turn it on? Some of the villagers noticed and started teasing us. "What's up? You're all so quiet after six weeks in town. Parents find a man for you? His tool too small?"

Hui was a shy girl who blushed easily, so she was the prime target. "Oh, I know," a young man said. "He confused you with your sister and slept with the wrong one. Heavens!"

The others took up his theme: "Very likely, who could tell the difference?"

Suddenly Hui exploded: "Is there an end to this or not?" She smashed her hoe on the ground in front of the young man.

This was so unusual for her that all the women immediately took Hui's part and chastised the young fellow, who protested he'd only been kidding.

I knew why Hui was so upset. It was nearly four o'clock and the sun was about to go down, but the PA system remained silent. Clearly all of us had failed.

The PA system was finally switched on to signal knocking-off time. Limper Lieu chose a local folk song called *Guilan Goes to University*:

> The rising red sun
> Sets the east aflame
> From the other side of the mountain
> Two come towards us
> An old man and his young daughter
> Old Zhang in his fifties,

And Guilan, very pretty
In her red top, black trousers and shoes made of cotton.
She is going to university.

By design or not, he kept playing this song well into the evening. I thought it was Lieu's way of telling us: "Stop dreaming! The university is still only open to workers, peasants and soldiers."

As soon as we got back home, Hui started wailing. "Do you know what pressure I'm under? Lan hasn't spoken to me for weeks. My parents keep telling me that she's the brainy one. It's so unfair."

Ying wiped away tears too.

I began to cook dinner. I was very sad, but my survival instincts had kicked in. I recalled all the humiliation and hardship I had endured, and ordered myself to accept my fate.

I had my own way of expressing my frustrations. The next morning, when the summoning bell rang, I announced firmly: "I'm not going to work today."

From the other room Hui echoed me immediately, "Me neither."

Then Ying's not-so-certain voice, "We're still on break after all."

Soon after, Chen came by with his shovel. We told him what we had decided and he joined us. We made breakfast together.

None of us had mastered the cooking range. When a villager lit a stove, the smoke was ducted through the hollow under the *kang*, whereas when we did it, the smoke just filled the rooms. We did not want to stay in our smoky room so after breakfast we went to brigade headquarters which Limper Lieu always kept clean and warm.

Limper Lieu sat on a chair at the broadcasting desk. There was a big stove between his chair and his bed. We three girls sat on his bed while Chen went back to his dormitory to drop off his shovel.

Lieu asked: "Why not go to work? Not happy? Really? Even the model graduate Ying? Surprise, surprise. I guess you all need to reflect."

Hui had enough of his sarcasm and went next door to the village co-op to buy a box of biscuits. "My treat, let's eat, and also you can shut your mouth, Limper Lieu."

Lieu picked up a biscuit and carried on: "No need to be unhappy. It's not that easy to become a university student! In ancient times, in village after village, maybe one in a hundred succeeded and not every year, once every *ten* years. Do you know what you just did? What you just did is called 'a toad desiring to eat a swan's flesh'."

Hui began to scream: "Spit it out – my biscuit, I mean." She jumped off the bed and went for him.

Lieu raised his arms to protect his face – "I haven't finished. I'm serious." Hui sat back down and he continued: "You won't be unhappy if you can reflect. Think about this: in this village, you are the swans. You have your special canteen and heating stoves in your rooms; when your tools are damaged or your stove is dead, we villagers are ordered to fix them. Think carefully: how often have you come here to ask for a piece of burned briquette? Which villager can make the same request? No one, only you can. So, why strive to be a fanciful toad when you can go on being a swan?"

We did not know how to react because his nonsense actually made sense. I said, "That's enough. Just give us a briquette and we'll go."

Lieu fetched his crutches and removed the kettle from the stove, checking to see if the top briquette was burning well or not. Just then the phone rang. He tried to move the kettle back quickly, to turn and to get back to the desk.

My heart was pounding. It suddenly occurred to me that the admission notice needed a day to get to the countryside. I grabbed the phone, "Hello?"

"Who are you?" a voice asked.

"One of the graduates," I said.

"Bring Limper Lieu to the phone, I need to talk to him."

Lieu had already moved back to his position, wagging his finger at me for my impudence in answering his phone.

Lieu took the phone and, putting on his official voice, said, "This is the headquarters of the brigade of the Village of Guests. I am Lieu … Ah, you are the commune education officer!"

We stared at him in deathly silence.

"May I ask, are you Officer Bai or Officer Zhang? Oh, Officer Zhang! I heard you had a holiday. How are your mother, your father, your wife and kids? Is the pig big enough to sell? What? You had to clean the pigsty again – such hard work."

He went on and on and we wanted to kick him. Finally he asked, "What do you want to tell me?" A long pause, then he nodded, "Mmm, mmm, right, is that so?"

Just then Chen walked in. We mimed madly at him that this was an important phone call. Now, the four of us, jumping up and down and moving around in the room, were waiting for the news. Then we heard, "Officer Zhang, you've got to be kidding. You are now sending me to Hell. How I am going to tell them that only two succeeded. You have no idea how vicious they are."

The atmosphere suddenly changed – we went quiet – two of us were going to be disappointed.

Finally Lieu shouted into the phone, "Okay, if you hear I'm dead, you'll know who did it!"

Hanging up, Limper Lieu turned around to face us. He was cold and emotionless. Pointing his crutches at Chen and at me, he said: "You and you – go and pack up. Tomorrow morning at ten, you're going to the commune office to get your admission notices and fill in all the forms. And you two," he turned to Hui and Ying, "sorry, you can only be swans in this village."

I remember nothing after that moment, neither Chen's and my response to the news nor the reactions of Hui and Ying. The rest of the day passed in a blur. That evening I had my farewell dinner at Immortal Zheng's home. His brother, our team leader Baolin, was there too. Everyone had a lot to say, but in my excitement, I didn't take anything in. Afterwards, I went to say goodbye to Driver Jinlin, Mingcheng, and Bing. Only Jinlin was at home and he congratulated me warmly. Both Mingcheng's and Bing's houses were in darkness.

The following day, Chen and I were like tops, spinning from the village to the commune, the commune to the village, back and forth four times. All kinds of official stamps were needed: the production brigade and the Communist branch committee of the Village of Guests had to release us; the commune military division had to cancel our membership in the local militia; the second and the first production teams had to prove we were no longer on their labour force; the commune's city graduates committee had to change our registration status, etc., etc. The party secretary, Mr Zhang, was so proud of us he lent us his official bike to do the rounds. Chen doubled me on the back. After multiple trips over four kilometres of bumpy dirt road, he had sore legs and I had a sore bottom.

We were both admitted to the first-rank Beijing Normal University, him for geophysics and me for literature. Five million, seven hundred thousand people had sat the exam and only 270,000 were admitted – less than 5 per cent – so we were the rarest of rarities and were congratulated by everyone we met, friends and strangers alike. By the time we had completed all the necessary formalities, we had fully realised our amazing achievement and were bursting with pride.

We were determined to take the evening bus home to tell our families the wonderful news as soon as possible. A long-distance phone call to Beijing was almost impossible and the mail was posted only once a week. There was no time to pack so we decided we would come back to collect our things later. Chen and I arranged to meet at the village entrance at 4:30 and walk together one more time that four-kilometre dirt road to the commune centre where we would catch the 5:30 bus. "Don't be late, otherwise we'll have to spend one more night here," Chen warned me.

When I got to the village entrance, I was astonished to see hundreds of villagers gathered under the two enormous Chinese scholar trees waiting to farewell us.

"Remember us, please," women said tearfully.

"Mention our village's name whenever you achieve anything," men urged us emotionally.

They thrust various gifts – eggs, peanuts, home-made sesame oil and dry sweet potatoes – into our travel bags. Chen was tearful, but I smiled non-stop because I was just so happy.

Finally Chen cried out his goodbyes and dragged me away. He didn't say a word till we reached the commune centre. "I thought you loved the village, we all thought so. But leaving them just now, you didn't seem to be sad at all." He sounded critical.

While I was trying to find words to explain my behaviour, the bus pulled into the other end of the commune centre. We ran to catch it.

We had just managed to sit down when the bus started moving. I turned my head to the window and suddenly saw Feng – she was running alongside the bus, holding a new diary and a pair of embroidered soles in one hand – her gift for me – and wiping away tears with the other. I waved and called out some parting words and watched her disappear in the dusk. She must have heard the news from her family so she slipped out of the factory and waited at the bus stop hoping to say goodbye to me. At that moment, my happiness gave way to sadness and loss. I sat back down and said to Chen, "I'm sorry. I've been too happy to think of the others. I've been really selfish."

From 20 October, the day I learnt about the exam, to 16 February, the day I left the Village of Guests, I had been totally preoccupied by preparing for the exam, and then with the results. What took place in my beloved village or among the other graduates, how Bing coped with his exam failure, and what was happening about Feng's projected marriage – all this fell by the wayside. Then, when I had gained a place at the university, everything happened quickly. I was too excited to think about Ying and Hui and what they were going through.

I was suddenly consumed by guilt that I had been so self-obsessed and indifferent to everyone else. I would carry that guilt with me always.

It was nearly 9 pm when I arrived home. I stopped on the front veranda and, through the inadequate curtains I had made five years before, saw my father and my brother Dong chatting with guests in the living room.

Two of them were neighbours: one was the boy who had lent me his father's records. He had not progressed beyond the first round in the exams and I heard him say: "Look, so far none of us has been successful. Do you realise that all nine of us are from bad families?"

My father agreed: "I noticed that a long time ago. Things can't change just like that. I'm still not sure hepatitis A was the real reason my son was rejected. That's why I was so angry with Xiyan when she wanted to study literature."

The other neighbour, the diplomat, comforted him, "Anyway, there's nothing to worry about now."

Just then, Dong saw me and quickly opened the door to let me in. "Xiyan's back," he announced. "Another loser, I guess." He picked up my bag: "Welcome to the losers' team. Don't be unhappy, we'll make it next year. Come and sit down."

I sat down, fetched out my admission notice and exclaimed. "You're wrong! I'm a university student now!"

There was a pause, a sudden silence as if no one could make sense of what I had just said. My father reacted first. He stood up and walked out of the room, but I couldn't tell if he was happy or angry to hear my news. Then everyone else jumped up, trying to grab the letter.

My brother got it first. "Oh, Heavens! It's Beijing Normal University, first rank!" He opened the door and shouted to the yard: "My sister is now a student of Beijing Normal University!"

The noise brought more people over – young and old – to have a look at the admission letter. Their faces were full of envy. Aunt Li called out my father: "Mr Bi, you're such a lucky man. Nine from our yard tried, only your daughter got it!"

My father finally came back out of his room. He looked happy now. He thanked the neighbours, took the letter from Dong, and read aloud: "Department of Chinese Language and Literature, Beijing Normal University – great choice. You know what?" He smiled to me. "This is the oldest university and your mother studied there when it used to be Furen University. She would certainly have approved of your choice."

Then I cried.

Afterword

Chen and I went back to the village to collect our luggage on 3 March, the last day of enrolment. We studied together in Beijing Normal University and remained good friends until he left for Germany with his fiancée in 1986. Our relationship could have been an intimate one if, in my single-minded pursuit of academic success, I had not turned a blind eye to his affections. A week before his departure, he revealed his unrequited love, wanting to know why I didn't like him. I had failed to pick up any signals, something I regretted for quite some time.

Hui gained university admission the following year. I learnt this from Ying, who failed the exam a second time but went on to become a model worker in a Beijing textile factories.

The other graduates remained in the village until the end of 1978, when the government formally ended the re-education policy. They were part of a phase in history known as the "Returning Home Movement".

I returned to the Village of Guests many times – as far as I know no one else did – but I never saw Feng and Bing again. Bing was regarded as a total loser because of his failed attempt to attend university. Even the girl with the blemished face refused to marry him, so he was reduced to becoming a live-in son-in-law whose children would bear his wife's surname and be cut off from his ancestral line, a great humiliation in rural China. Feng found a lover in the factory she worked in and decided to fight against the marriage that had been arranged for her. When the affair was exposed, she was condemned as a loose woman and ended up in an unhappy marriage to the man with the cleft palate. How their lives turned out continues to cause me grief. I continue to ask myself if I was responsible for their fates.

Driver Jinlin had an accident while transporting stones on a mountain road and suffered a spinal injury. I helped him to be admitted to the best Beijing hospital, but he never walked again. When I visited him the very last time in the spring of 1990, four years after his accident, we talked mainly about the shaft horse's foal – the best horse he had ever dealt with, even better than her mother, he said.

Immortal Zheng kept his word and made four beautiful quilts for me in 1987, for the wedding of my short-lived first marriage. He and his family continued to be protected by Heaven. In the time of the one-child policy and against the odds that there would be no grandson to continue the family line, his only son produced twins for him, a grandson and a granddaughter. I lost touch with this lovely family after leaving the country.

Third Daughter got married and had a daughter while I was studying at the university. When we met occasionally on weekends, she was always busy with housework. We never really spoke, just exchanging greetings. She eventually moved house and we lost contact.

Aunt Li opened her own business after China began opening its doors to the world in 1980. Her house backed onto Beihai Park so she turned her back wall into a kiosk and began selling food and drinks to the tourists. I cried when I heard that she died of cancer, in 1990. She was the one person who exemplified human decency in the most adverse situations of my life and she has been the inspiration for many of my stories.

Fourth Grandma returned to Beijing in 1980. She lived in our house, preparing my father's daily meals and spoiling Dong, Jing – who had also returned from the far northeast with his family – and me on the weekends when we visited. In November 1984, a week before the winter cabbage arrived, she lost our family's ration book (rationing continued until the 1990s). She didn't dare tell anyone but spent the whole day shuffling between the co-op and our house looking for it. She had a stroke that evening and died two weeks later. We eventually found the ration book – she had forgotten that she had hidden it under the table mat in the kitchen. I cried madly after her death, not only from grief but also in sorrow, for her life as concubine and servant, a life without choices. Twenty years later, I dedicated my novel *Born to Be a Concubine* to her.

In 1989, more than ten years after enrolling at university, I was living a very different life. After graduating from Beijing Normal University with a BA and an MA in classical Chinese language and literature, I taught at Renmin University in Beijing.

I had my own two-bedroom apartment, which in 1980s Beijing was almost a fairy tale. I decorated it stylishly, laying vinyl planks on the floor, and hanging tapestries and paintings on the walls.

I had stopped telling stories to neighbours and friends because books had become available again. The Chinese government lifted the literary ban in dramatic fashion: on 1 May 1978, bookshops across the nation began to sell reprints of classics, both Western and Chinese. People queued outside bookshops across the country from midnight on 30 April, so keen were they to buy this long-absent "spiritual food". I queued outside the main Xinhua Bookstore in the centre of Beijing for hours and bought Hugo's *Les Misérables*, Tolstoy's *Anna Karenina*, Balzac's *Le Père Goriot*, and Giovagnoli's *Spartacus* – not entirely by choice, more by whatever was available by the time I got to the counter. I spent a week's living expenses on them, but I felt rich because I had collected a treasure trove. The thrill I felt on being able to own those books is beyond description.

Every summer holiday I was on the road. I finished the Mount Emei climb and conquered Mount Hua; I hitchhiked from Sichuan to Tibet; I wandered along the border of China and the Soviet Union in the far northeast; I squeezed onto an ancient bus with peasants and their pigs, goats and roosters to cross over Great Mount Liang; I haggled with traders under the eyes of armed police on the street that straddled the border between China and British-governed Hong Kong.

By 1989, I had visited every corner of the "legendary landscape" in my illustrator neighbour's book. Back then, such a private travel record was almost unheard of in China. I was living an enviable life, but this was not enough. I wanted to go abroad.

After the government opened its doors in the mid-1980s, going abroad became possible. Many young intellectuals left the country, some sent by the government, others on foreign scholarships. I had done everything possible to win such an opportunity: I attended intensive English classes, I sat for TOEFL exams, and moonlighted to build up my funds, but it seemed that my major in classical Chinese literature excluded me. For the first time I felt that my father had been right to urge me to choose anything but literature.

Then hope reappeared. The Australian government was offering student visas and the chance to study English in private colleges for six months for about $5,000. This I could afford. Most university intellectuals thought this was beneath them as it didn't lead to a degree and it was not America, but I grabbed the opportunity. I applied to a college in Sydney and within a month had received an acceptance and a visa application form. What I needed to do next was get a permit of departure from Renmin University. There could be no passport without the backing of my workplace.

The news was bad. I was told I had to work five more years before I could be granted any leave – this was to repay my debt to the nation for nurturing and educating me. "Unless," the head of personnel said to me in jest, "you suddenly find a grandpa or an uncle in the foreign country you want to go to."

"Why?"

"That's the government's special policy for building healthy relationships with the outside world."

"How can I prove I have such a relative?"

"You need a letter of proof from an authority – at county level or above – with an official stamp on it. And the relative must be on your father's side."

My father was the son of a landlord from inland China. If you went back a hundred years you wouldn't find anyone from his family who had gone overseas. But I was not going to give up.

The democracy movement was taking shape in Tiananmen Square in the spring of 1989, influenced by reforms in the Soviet Union and Eastern Europe, and China was going through yet another period of political turmoil. Having grown up in Mao's China, always on the losing side, I feared mass movements and had little faith that current events would have a positive outcome. I had to get out now or I might never be able to follow in my mother's footsteps.

I spent the entire night thinking it through and by morning had formed a plan. I would go to my father's home district, Puren county in Henan province, and try to invent an Australian uncle. This mad plan was founded on two facts: my father's recent inclusion in the Historical Record of the Famous People of Puren County and an unusual gift I had received from a student.

I knew that villagers judged things less through the lens of party policies than through personal reactions, which, in most cases, sprang from a strong sense of kinship. Half of Puren county bore the surname Bi, and my father was a celebrity among them.

I had received an expensive gift from a friend, the daughter of the Japanese ambassador's driver, after I had helped her pass her exams. It was an electric shaver with a bottle of aftershave and a mirror with a silver frame, encased in an exquisite leather box – something not seen in 1980s China. I was sure this rare gift would astonish any official in Puren county.

Nevertheless, what I wanted to achieve was a crazy fantasy. I was not at all sure where it would lead and tried not to overthink it. I was a gambler staking everything on one throw – to get that official letter and go abroad!

After thirteen hours on a filthy train, I arrived at Puren county early in the morning. I found a public shower in the station square, washed and changed into an outfit more becoming of a lecturer. At 9 am, I walked into the Puren county office and asked to see the county magistrate. I mentioned my father's name and the receptionist immediately took me to the third floor and knocked on a door. The county magistrate, a man in his forties, invited me in. Thanks to my father's boasting, the magistrate knew everything about me – one of the first university graduates after the Cultural Revolution and, ten years later, a university lecturer.

As soon as he asked what he could do for me, I said point blank: "I want to go to Australia. But I'm not allowed to leave China for at least another five years unless I have a letter of proof from our county."

"To prove what?"

"That my uncle is in Australia and I'm going to visit him."

"Your uncle? In Australia?"

"Yes, my father's brother."

"Which one?"

"I don't know. That's why I need this letter of proof."

The magistrate looked at me and I stared back at him. After some seconds, he stood up: "I think my memory is not so good these days. Let's go down to ask the secretary to do a check." As he turned away from me, I read the expression on his face: "What is going on here?"

This was the moment to act. Once his secretary checked the records, my hopes would be shattered.

"Oh, I nearly forgot, I have something for you." I took a box from my bag. It was wrapped in old newspapers. "It's nothing, but it is from Beijing. I hate to trouble you like this."

"Well, you shouldn't have –" He took the little parcel and put it on his desk. "But since it's from Beijing, I accept it."

I followed the magistrate out of his room, down from the third level to the second, and from the second to the first, my heart sinking further with each level we descended. Suddenly he stopped. "I forgot something and have to go back to my office. Wait here. I'll be right back."

He is going back to check out the gift!

Almost ten minutes later, the county magistrate came down again: "Sorry to keep you so long. The phone kept ringing, people knocked on the door – anyway, I've got what I went for, the stamp of the county government. We'll need the stamp for the letter."

He wrote the letter of proof with a Chinese brush pen and in traditional vertical lines to lend it the proper formality. This uncle of mine now even had a name, Pin.

On 1 June 1990, I flew to Sydney on a half-empty Air China Boeing 747. Most of my fellow passengers were Chinese language students like myself. The excitement of going to a new country and fear of the unknown bound us strangers together and triggered a lively discussion on the plane. People shared in the triumph of getting to this stage and expressed their ambitions for life in Australia.

I went to the rear of the plane and stretched out in an empty row. No one would believe what I had done to get here because they had not had my history of facing challenges and taking risks. If I said that my ambition in Australia was to live as my mother had lived, I would be unable to describe what that was like.

I fell asleep and dreamed of my mother. She was reading a big dictionary in the living room of the family home. She looked much younger, with long permed hair and a slim-waisted jacket. "Look at this," she said, calling me over with the smile that I seldom saw. "It says here, 'A tree moves to its death but a person moves to a healthier life.' That's so true, isn't it?" She stood up and her smile vanished. "Except when a person backtracks. Read it –" she passed the dictionary to me.

I woke up. The lights were dimmed and the plane was quiet. I sat up and looked out the window and saw the stars were very bright. My omnipresent mother whose features had become blurred in my memory had set me on a never-ending quest. At every key moment in my life, she would let me know what she wanted. I interpreted her stylish appearance as a sign of her approval – I was no longer that ignorant girl who had no sense of style. However, her words in the dream sounded a caution: "Don't think this is your final leg! Plenty of choices lie ahead of you!"

*

I did not tell my father about my trip to his home town. I did not consult him about any of my decisions. He learnt of my first marriage two weeks before the wedding; and I gave him short notice of my move to Australia. We maintained a peaceful relationship. I visited home regularly and carried out my daughterly duties, first from my student dormitory and then from my own apartment. We discussed literature and current affairs but never talked about the past.

A year after moving to Sydney, I bought a sheep skin and posted it to him. It was July, a hot summer in Beijing. He was overjoyed, Dong told me, and wore the sheepskin around the yard to show off to the neighbours. Dong joked: "In future, you'd better consider the season. Our father nearly had heatstroke."

My father wrote me many letters, enclosing poems, literary anecdotes and bits of folklore that he knew I would enjoy. These were loving gestures. When he died at the end of 1991 I was not at his deathbed.

I learnt about his death a week later, prompted by a dream in which he came to me in Sydney. He looked tired and said, "You're so far away. It's taken me a week to get here to say goodbye." When I woke up, I rang my brother Dong – I knew my father had cancer. Dong said: "We didn't have a chance to tell you. Our father passed away a week ago." Hours before he died, Dong said, he kept asking that some change be put into his pockets. "I need to travel a lot and I need to see your mother. I have to be ready."

His last words – which I interpreted as his last effort to reconcile with me and my mother – altered my opinion of him. I had been so convinced that his past wrongs to his wife and daughter were unforgivable. But after he died I kept reminding myself that we were all who we were and did what we did because we had lived in China during the Mao years. I couldn't help wondering: *Would any of these things have happened in another, more normal, time?*

The ten years of my father's exile was never a topic of conversation between us. We don't know what he endured in the desert. But a casual remark he made one day about his knowledge of Beijing Opera gave Dong and me a glimpse of his suffering: "I'm glad I can sing the scores of so many operas. Whenever they had me on the stage being denounced, bent over at the waist with my arms stretched back, I would sing operas in my head. I'd be fully involved in the plot so the pain would ease and the time passed quickly. That's why I rarely fainted on the stage."

He must have been overjoyed to learn that he could go back to Beijing "rehabilitated". Could I blame him for not delaying his homecoming? During the Cultural Revolution, policies changed so frequently that people had no faith in the government. What if things had changed back in those three months? This thought must have crossed his mind.

I don't defend him for writing that damning letter to the commune. But I must acknowledge that injustice can make people bitter.

In September 2014, four of us – my second-oldest brother, Shu, fourth-oldest brother, Dong, my fifth-oldest brother, Jing, and me – met in Xi'an and talked over many of the old family dramas. My oldest brother, Yang, was in Vienna, participating in an international choir competition. My third-oldest brother, Ning, had died five years earlier in a car accident.

I used the opportunity to ask a question I had long brooded over: "Why did no one bother about me after Mum's death?" It was then I learnt the others' survival stories.

After my mother's funeral, Shu and Dong assumed responsibility for paying back the money that they had borrowed from colleagues for Ning's and Jing's return to Beijing. They had also raised 22 yuan for their trips back to their respective communes. "Dong and I were completely absorbed in the task of calculating money, day in day out, and could do nothing about anything else," Shu said.

Ning was given 14 yuan for his 65-yuan train trip to Khashgar. His money ran out when he got to Dunhuang, at the start of the Silk Road. He was arrested for harming national pride as he busked for foreign tourists in an attempt to raise money to get back to Khashgar. He was only able to eventually reach his destination through the help of one kind woman.

With the 8 yuan given to him, Jing managed to get as far as Tangshan, which did not even get him out of Hebei province. He exchanged labour on the way for his fare to the far northeast. When he finally arrived at Baichengzi he found it buried in snow. There was not a single road sign to be seen. He trekked for hours from the little train station and ended up completely lost. "It was dark and cold. I thought it was the end and pretty much gave up." Luckily, two city graduates from the neighbouring village who had come out to steal a chicken found him lying in the snow. They took him to their dormitory and saved his life.

For a long time, I felt angry because everyone had abandoned me. But now I know that we all had to fight our own battles during those extremely difficult years. Only now, from this distance, can I judge the others more fairly. None of us emerged unscathed from that extraordinarily dark time.

I should definitely say something about my mother. After all, it was her last words that drove me for so many years and, doubtless, will never cease driving me. But she died so early and was so efficient in erasing her past that I cannot be sure how much of her "rich and worthy life" is all in my imagination.

What I remember about her does not support that image. She was often frustrated or depressed; nothing about her life was enviable. I have tried hard to recall a moment when I saw her happy, and can only find one. She is sitting on the veranda, playing the *erhu* for the neighbours. When she finishes, everyone applauds and she laughs out loud. I must have been very young because I don't have any idea when or why that happened.

But I know my vision of her is not wrong.

In 2004, I made a special trip to Taiyuan to visit Aunt Yuqin, my mother's only surviving sibling. Apparently, in 1930 my mother was a young Westernised student, a smoker, a drinker with lots of friends. She fell madly in love with a handsome young man but in the end he refused to marry her.

"Why?"

"She was not pretty enough for him," Aunt Yuqin said, matter-of-factly. "She was broken-hearted and left home the next day. We didn't hear from her for many years, until after she married your father. She never told us what she did during those years."

My parents married in 1938, so there are eight lost years in my mother's life. She might, as the stories had it, have travelled in China, studied abroad, organised anti-Japanese street propaganda in Shanghai, or worked as a secretary in the headquarters of the Kuomintang Eighth Group Army in Wuhan. Or she might have done none of these things since no one can verify them.

One thing was clear from talking to Aunt Yuqin. My father's looks must have played a role in their marriage. He was a handsome man, tall, straight, with large eyes and a fair complexion, and he didn't find my mother's appearance wanting.

My mother had lived through a turbulent and transitional China. Born in the year of Dr Sun Yat-sen's revolution (1911), educated under the influence of the New Culture Movement, having struggled through the war with Japan and the war between the Kuomintang and the Communists, she embraced the new China. Even with her unfortunate domestic situation, she had managed to live happily and meaningfully as a union leader. This I knew from Immortal Zheng, and Yang and Shu, my two oldest brothers, confirmed this. They often heard my mother recite Maxim Gorky's "The Song of the Storm Petrel", which tells how the big bird joyfully flaps its wings through the storms while other birds cower. But in her last few years, I often heard her sing an aria from a Beijing Opera:

> I am a bird locked in a cage,
> with my wings I cannot fly;
> I am a goose come from the south,

cut off from my flock,
I have lost my way;
I am a tiger who left the mountain,
I endure on a hostile plain;
I am a dragon run aground,
trapped and stranded in the sand.

When my mother came to the end of her life, she began to despair for her daughter, born into a wrong time, without a chance of even knowing it! In that dark period, not many had a vision of light. If I were her, I might also have felt lucky and not feared death.

I didn't "backtrack" and I settled in Australia. I became a teacher and a published writer, mastered English and started to learn French. I have listened to my mother and kept embracing new choices.

I share my life with a husband who loves books, a son who is crazy about birds, a golden retriever and three domestic short-haired cats whom I worship for their alert, unsentimental and independent approach to life. I am far away from my childhood home and the Village of Guests but my past is always with me.

One day I hope my mother appears in my dreams again, sitting with me on my sun-drenched veranda, drinking coffee as we watch the goldfish swim in the pots and ponds of my garden, both of us relaxed and pleased where my life has brought me, so far.

Left to right: (Vivian) Xiyan's five brothers: Jing, Dong, Shu, Yang, Ning, and Xiyan
Taken at Beijing's Summer Palace, Spring 1965

www.ingramcontent.com/pod-product-compliance
Ingram Content Group UK Ltd.
Pitfield, Milton Keynes, MK11 3LW, UK
UKHW041950190726
13854UKWH00004B/1881

9 781925 736106